100 Simple Bible Crafts

100 Simple Bible Crafts

Sue Price

Eastbourne

First published 1998
Reprinted 1999, 2001, 2002, 2004

New edition 2007
1 2 3 4 5 6 7 Print/Year 09 08 07

ISBN 978-1-842912-92-8

Designed by PinnacleCreative.co.uk

Published by
Kingsway Communications Ltd
Lottbridge Drove, Eastbourne BN23 6NT, England.
Email: childrensministry@kingsway.co.uk

Printed in the USA

CONTENTS

SECTION TWO: LESSON REMINDER CRAFTS 75

SECTION THREE: WORSHIP CRAFTS   137

SECTION FOUR: CRAFTS TO GIVE   179

SECTION FIVE: SEASONAL CRAFTS   201

ACKNOWLEDGEMENTS

Is any craft idea truly original? Some of these ideas I have used and adapted over the years and cannot recall their original source. Others I believe I have created for this book. However, I know from experience that what you believe is an original idea may already be in use by someone else.

I would acknowledge that some of these ideas have been developed from crafts originally appearing in Bible-in-Life curricula and I am indebted to Audrey Milton for the 'Candle curtains' (idea no. 76). Beyond that I would apologise to anyone who thinks they are the original source for any of the other crafts. I have not knowingly or intentionally copied their idea.

My thanks go to Ruth and Hannah, who spent much of their Easter holidays making these ideas, checking that my instructions work in practice. Of course, if any instruction is confusing or wrong, I apologise—the responsibility is mine.

Sue Price

INTRODUCTION

Many of us, but especially children, learn more effectively when there is a visual stimulus and the opportunity to interact with the lesson. Crafts should therefore be regarded as an important element of any session with children—not just an add-on. The children will remember what they see and what they experience much better than what they are told.

This book contains craft ideas that will help children learn Bible stories and verses, and that will assist them in expressing those Bible truths in their own lives and in their relationships with others. I have set each craft in a learning context, but in my own experience I have found that a book of crafts is usually just the starting point. You may carry out the instructions to the letter once, to be sure you understand the method, but next time you will modify the activity to better suit your own circumstances. You may just change the materials used or you may take the basic idea and adapt it for a different story. I would encourage you to individualise the ideas in this book and make them work for you and your children. Because of this I have not given age guidelines for the ideas in the book. As presented here, they should all be achievable by most 7- to 11-year-olds and many will be achievable by younger children. With help during the session or with some advance preparation, even pre-school children should be able to attempt a large number of the projects.

The first section of the book contains ideas that enable children to interact with a story, and some of these are particularly appropriate for younger children. If you wish to provide hands-on visual aids for very young children or toddlers, you could construct these crafts totally in advance of the lesson.

The book is divided into five sections:

- *Story Crafts* will provide you with simple ideas that enable children to interact with a story as you tell it.
- *Lesson Reminder Crafts* will help children recall Bible truths or their life application through the coming week.
- *Worship Crafts* will give a visual stimulus for times of praise or prayer.
- *Crafts to Give* are ideas based on Bible themes that provide opportunities to share lessons or evangelise to friends or family.
- *Seasonal Crafts* provide Bible-based ideas for the festivals of Christmas, Valentine's Day and Easter.

Every craft in this book has a Bible reference, or relates more generally to a group of stories, but several can be used directly, or with minor modifications, with other Bible passages. Just two examples are 'The boat in a storm' (no. 20), which would be just as appropriate for Paul's missionary journeys, and 'Helpful hands' (no. 56), which could apply to any story that was being used to show how God wants us to help others.

While encouraging you to adapt and develop the crafts in this book, I would suggest there are two things you should always consider before you use an idea. First, will the craft help children to understand the focus of my session? If the project doesn't reinforce the story, the Bible truth or its life application, don't include it, however much fun it seems.

Second, have I made sure that the project will be achievable by each group member? Frustration due to the craft being too hard will more than negate the benefits of interactive learning. Know the abilities of your children and either do some advance preparation or be prepared to give extra assistance to individuals in the group who struggle. Generally choose projects that are within the capabilities of all the children—you can always add elements, such as background detail or more decoration, for those quick to finish. There will almost always be as much learning benefit from a simple craft as from a complicated one.

100 Simple Bible Crafts

Section One:
STORY CRAFTS

These are generally simple ideas that enable children to interact with a story. Most of the ideas need to be completed, or at least started, in advance of the story time and so they could provide an activity for children to do as they arrive. Do, however, have a couple already made up so that late-comers are not excluded during the story (they will also be useful to show the children what the completed craft should look like). Taking the craft home will also have it act as a lesson reminder.

   With pre-school children you may prefer to make the craft in advance and use it as an interactive visual aid during the story time.

CREATION STORY-WHEEL

Bible reference: Genesis 1

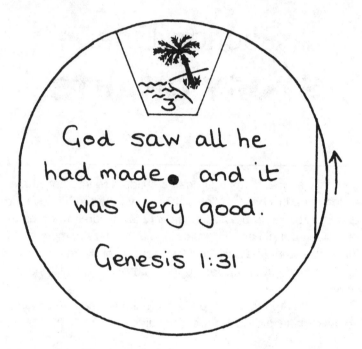

God saw all he
had made. and it
was very good.
Genesis 1:31

Each child will need
- 2 circles of card approximately 14cm in diameter
- a paper-fastener
- scissors, a ruler and felt pens

In advance of the story time

Divide one circle into seven equal segments (for a 14cm circle the length across the top of each segment is barely 6cm). Find and mark the centre of the second circle. Mark a point on the circumference, then measure and mark 5.5cm across the circumference from that first point. From each of these points in turn, place the ruler joining them to the centre of the circle and draw a line 4cm down from the edge. Draw a third line joining the ends of these two lines. Cut out this section. With the cut-out section pointing upwards, cut a narrow slice off the right-hand side of the disc (left-hand side for left-handed children).

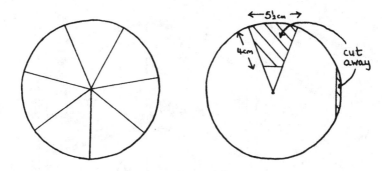

Place the first circle behind the second and fix the two together using the paper-fastener through their centres. Rotate the back circle so that the cut-out section reveals one of the seven segments. Write '1' at the bottom of this revealed section. Continue to rotate the circle clockwise, marking the subsequently revealed sections '2', '3', '4', '5', '6' and '7'.

As the story is told

Stop at the end of each day and have the children draw a simple representation of the created element (ensuring the first day is in the section marked '1', etc.). On the seventh day encourage them to think of a way to represent God resting. Finally, write the Bible verse on the front circle.

Bible verse: 'God saw all that he had made, and it was very good' (Genesis 1:31).

CREATION COLLAGE BOOKLET

Bible reference: Genesis 1

This is a craft that is ideally suited for a review lesson after a series of lessons looking at creation.

Each child will need
- 8 large-paged scrap-book sheets*
- pictures cut from magazines and catalogues
- scissors, glue and felt pens

* Remove the staples from a cheap scrap-book and divide it into two double sheets per child. Either re-staple the pages with a long-arm stapler or stitch them for each child.

In advance of the story time
Write '[child's name]'s Creation Book' on the front cover. Divide each of the six inside pages in half, top and bottom.

As the story is told
On the top half of each page write and illustrate, either with drawings or cut-out pictures, what was created on the first, second, third, fourth, fifth and sixth day.

After the story
On the bottom half of each page come up with six suggestions (which may be influenced by the pictures you have managed to collect) such as 'orange things God created', 'blue things God created', 'scrumptious things God created', 'scary things God created' or 'stars God created' (this last giving the children the opportunity to include pictures of their pop or sporting heroes). Older children should write the Bible verse on the back cover to remind them that God rested on the seventh day and wants us to keep one day of the week special for him.

Bible verse: 'If you keep your feet from breaking the Sabbath and from doing as you please on my holy day, if you call the Sabbath a delight and the Lord's holy day honourable, and if you honour it by not going your own way and not doing as you please or speaking idle words, then you will find your joy in the Lord' (Isaiah 58:13).

ANIMAL MASKS

Bible reference: Genesis 7:1–10

Each child will need
- a paper plate
- a piece of card approximately 10cm × 12cm
- thin elastic
- scissors, glue, felt pens, paints, a brush and a stapler

In advance of the story time

Choose an animal and, if it needs ears, draw them on the card, cut them out and staple them to the paper plate to form the face. Hold the plate in front of the face and mark where the eye holes will need to be cut. Use paint and/or felt pens to colour and add features to the face, then carefully cut out the eye holes. Staple the elastic to one side of the mask, level with the eye holes. Hold the mask to the face and measure the length of elastic needed for a comfortable fit. Cut and staple the elastic to the other side of the mask.

As the story is told

The children can wear their masks throughout the story time. Ask them how the animals might have felt all herded together on the ark and how they think Noah would have treated the animals.

––––––––––––––––––––––––– TIP –––––––––––––––––––––––––

Paper plates are an excellent way of providing circles and semi-circles of card.

THUMBPRINT ANIMALS

Bible reference: Genesis 7:1–10

Each child will need
- an A3 sheet of paper
- a silhouette ark, cut out of black paper, approximately 20cm × 15cm
- a stamp pad of black paint*
- glue and a black pen
- warm, soapy water and a towel

* Make the stamp pad using a deep-sided lid (from a coffee jar or similar) with several layers of paper towel folded inside. Pour on a very small quantity of thick black paint.

As the story is told
Allow the children to build up the picture as the story develops. As Noah builds the ark, stick on the silhouette near the top of the paper. As Noah collects and loads the animals onto the ark, have the children create their collage by using thumb- and fingerprints to form the bodies and heads of animals. Add details with a black pen. Encourage them to make pairs of each animal.

JACOB AND ESAU PUPPET

Bible reference: Genesis 27:1–40

Each child will need
- a piece of card approximately 20cm × 12cm
- a drinking straw
- red wool
- material scraps—including some fake fur, or other material with a raised pile, in a neutral colour
- a puppet template (see page 222)
- sticky tape, glue and felt pens

In advance of the story time
Draw round the template on the card and cut out the puppet. Flatten one end of the straw and use sticky tape to attach about half the straw to the cut-out so that the puppet can be held upright. On one side of the puppet create Esau: cut to size and stick fake fur fabric onto the arms, appropriate material for a tunic and wool for his hair and beard. Add other features with felt pens. On the other side of the puppet create Jacob: cut to size and stick material for a tunic and a head-dress. Leave the arms smooth and add other features with felt pens.

As the story is told
The children can turn the puppet to show which brother is being referred to throughout the story. When Jacob goes to Isaac disguised as Esau they can use the Esau side of the puppet. Talk about the differences between Jacob and Esau and how Jacob managed to deceive his father.

———————————————————— TIP ————————————————

Whenever card of an unspecified colour is required throughout this book, cereal packets would be appropriate.

_____

JOSEPH AND HIS BROTHERS

Bible reference: Genesis 29:31–30:24; 35:23–26

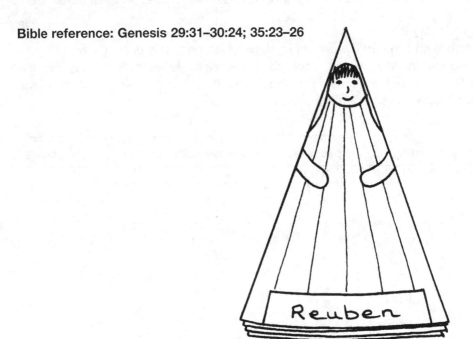

This set of 'Russian dolls' can be used with any of the stories referring to Joseph and his brothers.

Each child will need
- photocopied sheets with the 12 figures to be cut out*
- scissors, sticky tape or glue, and felt pens

* Draw the master sheets with twelve cone outlines in decreasing sizes. Each cone outline should be one-third of a circle, plus a flap for sticking (the cone radii being 5cm, $5\frac{1}{3}$cm, $5\frac{2}{3}$cm, 6cm, $6\frac{1}{3}$cm, $6\frac{2}{3}$cm, 7cm, $7\frac{1}{3}$cm, $7\frac{2}{3}$cm, 8cm, $8\frac{1}{3}$cm and $8\frac{2}{3}$cm). Draw a simple figure outline on each cone—head at the tip, arms, striped tunic and a rectangle where the brother's name can be added at the base.

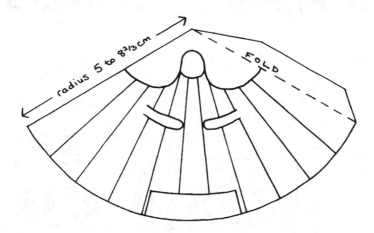

In advance of the story time

Add the brothers' names to the cones before they are cut out so that the order is still easily identified. The largest cone is Reuben and then Simeon, Levi, Judah, Dan, Naphtali, Gad, Asher, Issachar, Zebulun, Joseph and finally Benjamin, the smallest. Cut out each figure and colour them differently, giving Joseph the most brightly coloured coat. Form into a cone shape and stick.

The children may work in groups, at least before the story time, to create a set of twelve brothers. They could then have the opportunity to make the remainder of their set later on in the session time.

As the story is told

The figures can be used during the story time. They can then be stacked from smallest to largest, like Russian dolls, and saved for further episodes of the Joseph story.

TV STORY BOX—JOSEPH AND PHARAOH'S DREAMS

Bible reference: Genesis 41

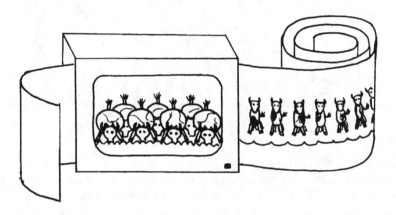

Each child will need
- a cardboard box approximately 10cm × 7cm × 3cm (this is the approximate size of a box containing a tin of sardines). If you cannot collect appropriate boxes, make them from card, adjusting the outline shown for craft no. 68. Follow the instructions for making up the brick, but don't stick down flaps E and F
- a strip of paper 85cm × 6cm (the exact size of this paper depends on your box size—the length should be the length of the box less 1cm, multiplied by 9, plus 4cm and the width should be the width of the box less 1cm)
- scissors, a ruler, sticky tape and felt pens (plus paints or coloured paper to decorate the box if you wish)

In advance of the story time

Draw a 'screen' on one side of the box, leaving a margin of 1cm all the way round. If your box has tuck-in flaps at either end, keep the sides that open nearest the 'screen' (these are flaps E and F if you are constructing your own box). If the box is sealed, slit all the way along the end edges nearest the 'screen'. Cut out the screen and then decorate the box to look like a TV set. Divide your strip of paper into sections, drawing lines 2cm from the edge and then every 9cm (adjust this distance if your box is not 10cm long), leaving 2cm at the end. You should have nine sections plus the two margins.

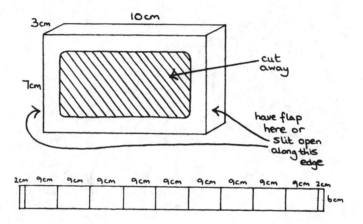

As the story is told

Starting with the first section of the paper strip, draw scenes to represent the following nine key points in the story: v.14, v.18, v.19, vv.22–23, v.24, vv.28–31, vv.41–43, vv.47–49 and vv.55–56.

After the story

Thread the paper strip through the flaps or slits at either end of the box so that the pictures pass behind the 'television screen'. Gently pull the strip through, revealing the pictures in turn and retelling the story.

THE RED SEA DIVIDE

Bible reference: Exodus 14:21–28

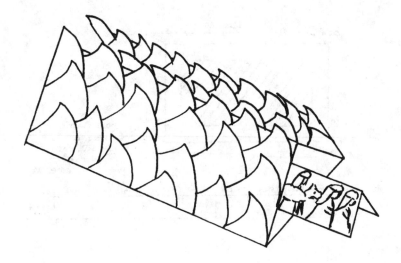

Each child will need
- an A4 sheet of card
- a piece of card approximately 20cm × 10cm
- blue tissue paper
- scissors, a ruler, glue and felt pens

In advance of the story time

Divide the A4 piece of card into four sections lengthways. Score the two outer lines so that the outer quarters fold in to cover the centre section. Cut wave shapes out of the blue paper and stick them onto the outer quarters of the card—both front and back.

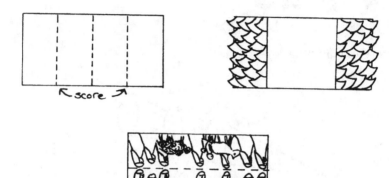

Divide the other piece of card in half lengthways. Score this line so that the card can be folded to form a long inverted V-shape. Draw simple figures of people and animals along both sides of the 'V', all facing the same direction, with heads to the point of the 'V'.

As the story is told

Start with the waves folded over the centre section. As God parts the sea, open the waves to reveal the sea-bed and push across the people and their animals.

JERICHO WALLS AND TRUMPETS

Bible reference: Joshua 6:1–20

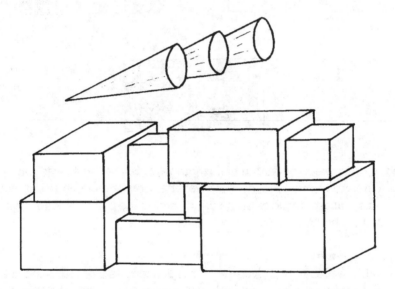

Each child will need
- a piece of thin card or thick paper (possibly ridged or textured paper that is representative of horn) approximately 30cm × 20cm
- scissors and sticky tape

In addition, the whole group will require a collection of large cardboard boxes.

In advance of the story time

Draw a conical outline (a third of a circle with a 20cm radius) on the card or paper. Cut it out, roll it into a trumpet shape and fix with sticky tape. Build a wall of cardboard boxes.

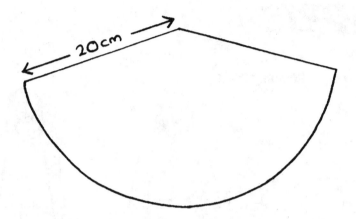

As the story is told

If you have seven or less in your group, have each child play the part of the priests at every point in the story. If you have more than seven in the group, swap children around to play the priests. On the seventh day involve all the children—seven priests and the rest of the people who shout. Allow the children to knock down the 'wall' of boxes.

DAVID AND JONATHAN PUPPETS

Bible reference: 1 Samuel 18:1–4

Each child will need
- a piece of card approximately 20cm × 20cm
- a piece of paper approximately 20cm × 12cm
- a puppet template (see page 222)
- 2 drinking straws
- scissors, sticky tape and felt pens

In advance of the story time

Draw round the template onto the card twice and cut out the two figures. Flatten one end of each straw and use sticky tape to attach about half the straws to the figures so that the puppets can be held upright. Colour in the figures to represent David and Jonathan wearing tunics, not robes.

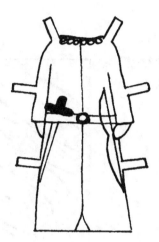

Draw round the template onto the paper and use the outline to draw a robe with a belt, a sword tucked into the belt and a bow being held in front of the robe. Either side of where the head is on the template, and on either side of the sleeves and lower robe, add tabs 0.5cm wide and 2cm long. Cut round this new outline and colour in the robe. Use the tabs to fix the robe onto Jonathan.

As the story is told

At the appropriate time move the robe from Jonathan to David.

ELIJAH TAKEN TO HEAVEN

Bible reference: 2 Kings 2:11–12

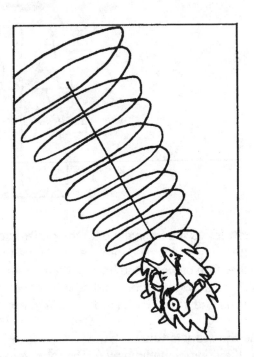

Each child will need
- an A4 sheet of card
- a piece of yellow card approximately 10cm × 6cm
- a piece of orange paper approximately 8cm × 4cm
- cotton—approximately 30cm long
- scissors, sticky tape, glue and felt pens

In advance of the story time

Round the corners of the yellow card to an oval, then draw flame shapes all pointing in one direction—towards a narrow end of the oval—and cut out. Draw a horse pulling a chariot with Elijah inside on a piece of orange paper that will fit inside the yellow card shape. Roughly cut round the horse and chariot. Stick the horse, chariot and Elijah onto the yellow card.

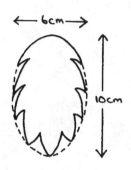
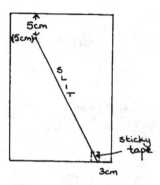

Cut a slit in the A4 piece of card that starts 3cm in from the lower right-hand corner and finishes 5cm in and 5cm down from the upper left-hand corner. Use a 4cm length of sticky tape, folded over the lower edge of the card, to close the bottom end of the slit. Draw ovals of increasing size spiralling up round the slit to represent a whirlwind. Stick both ends of the cotton to the back of the yellow card—one at either end—and then pull the loop of cotton through the slit. Position the chariot at the bottom of the slit.

As the story is told

At the appropriate time move Elijah towards heaven by pulling the cotton from the back.

NAAMAN—HAPPY AND SAD FACES

Bible reference: 2 Kings 5:1–14

Each child will need
- a paper plate
- a craft stick
- wool
- sticky tape and felt pens

In advance of the story time
Use sticky tape to attach the craft stick to the paper plate, forming a handle. Draw a sad face on one side (include 'blotches' representing the leprosy suffered by Naaman). Draw a happy face on the other side of the plate. Stick wool round the top of the plate, falling down both sides to represent hair.

As the story is told
The sad face represents Naaman during the first part of the story, and the happy face shows how he felt after he was cured.

––––––––––––––––––––––––––––––––––– TIP ––––––––––––––––––––––––––––––––––––
Craft sticks are like ice-lolly sticks, which you could collect and use instead.

JOASH'S CROWN

Bible reference: 2 Kings 12

Each child will need
- a strip of card or thick paper approximately 60cm × 12cm
- various pieces of brightly coloured and shiny paper (e.g. sweet wrappers)
- scissors, glue and a stapler

In advance of the story time
Measure the card or paper around the child's head and mark where it needs to
be joined for the crown to fit snugly. Cut the strip, leaving a 1–2cm overlap.
(Optional: cut a zigzag pattern for the top of the crown.) Stick scrunched-up
coloured paper onto the crown to look like jewels. You could give each child one
brightly wrapped sweet to stick on as a gem at the centre of the crown (halfway
along the strip of card or paper), which they could eat at the end of the lesson or
when they go home. Staple the strip as marked to form the crown.

As the story is told
The children can wear their crowns throughout the story to remind them that
Joash was a child king who did good things for God.

JEREMIAH'S SCROLL

Bible reference: Jeremiah 36

Each child will need
- a strip of paper approximately 30cm × 8cm
- a drinking straw
- scissors, sticky tape and felt pens

In advance of the story time
Cut the straw in half. Use sticky tape to attach either end of the paper strip to the two halves of the straw so that the paper will roll up round them. Roll up most of the strip around one half of the straw and the remainder around the other so that the two halves of the straw lie side by side.

At the end of the story
The children may write as many Bible stories as they can think of that God would have told Jeremiah to include on the scroll.

FIERY FURNACE PUPPETS AND STREAMERS

Bible reference: Daniel 3

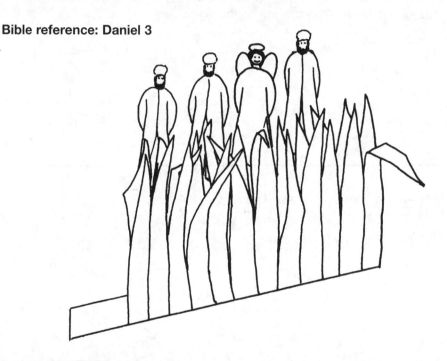

Each child will need
- 2 strips of thick card 20cm × 2cm
- 4 pieces of card 9cm × 3.5cm, with the corners rounded at one end
- a craft stick
- yellow and orange tissue paper
- scissors, sticky tape and felt pens

In advance of the story time

On three of the four pieces of card draw and colour Shadrach, Meshach and Abednego in robes, trousers and turbans. On the fourth piece of card draw an angel. Cut a 1cm slot up from the centre base of each figure.

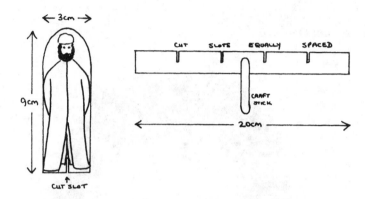

Cut four equally spaced 1cm slots in one of the long sides of a strip of card. Using sticky tape, attach the craft stick to the centre of this strip so that it can be held with the slots uppermost. Cut twenty-four 'flames' from tissue paper, each 10–12cm long with a base width of 1cm tapering to nothing. Leaving 4–5cm at one end of the second strip of card, stick the bases of twelve 'flames' side by side along one face of the strip and the other twelve 'flames' backing on to them along the other face.

As the story is told

Slot the three figures of Shadrach, Meshach and Abednego into three of the slots on the holder at the start of the story. Shake the flames to represent the furnace and add the figure of the angel to accompany the friends as they pass behind the flames.

LION MASKS

Bible reference: Daniel 6

Each child will need
- a piece of yellow or light brown card, approximately 30cm × 20cm, pre-drawn with the mask outline
- yellow, orange and brown wool cut into 5–8cm lengths
- thin elastic
- scissors, glue, felt pens and a stapler

In advance of the story time
Cut out the mask. Hold it in front of the face and mark where the eye holes need to be cut. Cut out the eye holes and draw on other features such as the nose and mouth. Starting at the top, and working in sections of approximately 5cm at a time, spread glue on the outer 2–3cm of the mask and then stick lengths of wool side by side, overlapping the edge of the mask, to form the mane. (The jagged outline of the mask means that, as long as the sections are worked equally down both sides of the mask, it will still look effective, even if only about one third of the mane is completed.) Staple one end of the elastic to one side of the mask, level with the eyes. Measure the elastic around the head, cut it to the required length and staple the other end to the other side of the mask.

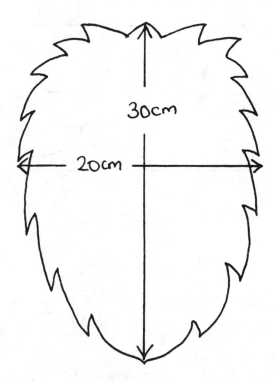

As the story is told
When Daniel is thrown to the lions the children can put on their masks. Ask them how they think the lions would usually have behaved. How *did* they behave? Why do they think the lions behaved in the way they did?

JONAH AND THE FISH

Bible reference: Jonah 1:15–17

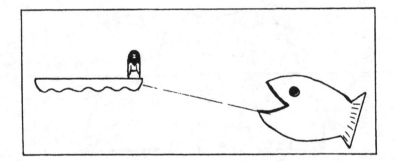

Each child will need
- a piece of blue card 50cm × 20cm
- 3 strips of card: 30cm × 0.5cm, 4cm × 0.5cm and 6cm × 2cm
- brown and grey paper, each piece approximately 15cm × 10cm
- scissors, sticky tape, glue and felt pens

In advance of the story time

Cut a slit in the card starting 2cm up from the lower right-hand corner and ending 10cm from the top and 15cm in from the left-hand edge. Use a 4cm length of sticky tape folded over the edge of the card to close the end of the slit. Cut a simple boat shape approximately 15cm long from the brown paper and a simple fish shape, with its mouth open and approximately 15cm long by 10cm wide, from the grey paper.

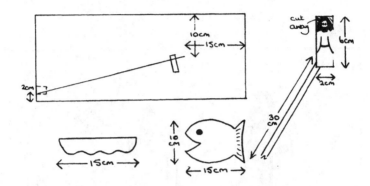

Stick the boat onto the card so that its top right-hand end just covers the top 2cm of the slit (do not stick the boat down above the slit). Position the fish in the bottom right-hand corner of the card so that the slit runs into the lower side of the mouth. Only stick the edges of the fish, leaving the mouth free. On the 6cm × 2cm piece of card draw and colour Jonah. Round off the corners at the head end. With Jonah upright, stick the long strip of card to the back of Jonah at an angle that forms seven o'clock. Position the shorter strip onto the back of the blue card 2cm from the top end of the slit, with 1cm above the slit and 3cm below the slit. Only stick down the ends, leaving the centre 2cm free.

As the story is told

At the start of the story insert Jonah through the slit from the back of the card so that he is standing in the boat. As the story unfolds, using the long strip, tilt him to almost horizontal and then gently push him across the sea until he is swallowed by the fish.

JOHN BAPTISES JESUS

Bible reference: Matthew 3:13–17

Each child will need
- an A4 sheet of green card
- 2 card figures approximately 12cm × 5cm
- a piece of blue paper 10cm × 30cm
- a square of white paper approximately 5sq. cm
- a paper-fastener
- scissors, glue and felt pens

In advance of the story time
Colour in the figures. Draw peaks of waves along one long side of the blue paper and cut them out. Stick the figure of John 5cm from the left-hand edge of the card with the base 5cm up from the bottom. Position the figure of Jesus to the right of John, 14cm from the left-hand edge of the card and 4cm up from the bottom.

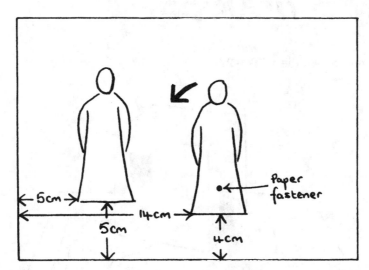

Fix the Jesus figure to the card background with the paper-fastener 2.5cm up from the base and midway between the two sides of the figure. Place the blue paper to cover the lower 10cm of the card. Stick down 1cm along the bottom edge and 2cm down each side. Cut a dove from the white paper.

As the story is told
Rotate the figure of Jesus so that he lies in the water with his head by John. After he is raised out of the water again, stick the dove onto the picture close to his head.

WISE AND FOOLISH MEN'S HOUSES

Bible reference: Matthew 7:24–27

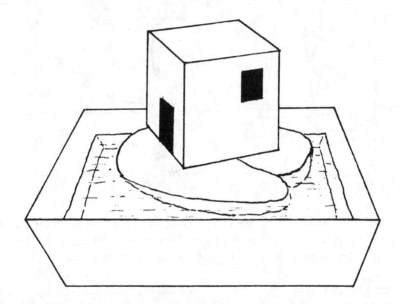

Each child will need
- a piece of card 29cm × 23cm
- scissors, glue and felt pens

For the story you will also need a tray that will hold water about 2cm deep, some flat stones, some rice and a jug of water.

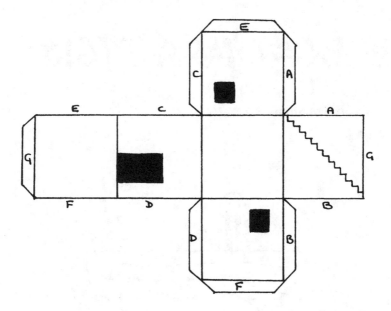

In advance of the story time

Draw the net for the house onto the card—each side is 7cm and the flaps are 1cm wide—and cut it out. Score all the lines to be folded. Draw features on the house (door, windows and stairs) and then make up the cube by sticking all the flaps under the faces as marked and in the order indicated (A through to G).

As the story is told

For the wise builder, place in the tray some flat stones that will sit out of 2cm of water. Place a house on the stones, pour water into the tray (not directly over the house) to about 2cm and let the children swirl it around. The house will stand firm, out of the water. For the foolish builder, heap a pile of rice about 3cm high in the centre of the tray. Place a house onto the pile of rice. Again pour water into the tray and let the children swirl it around. This time the rice pile and the house will collapse into the water.

THE BOAT IN A STORM

Bible reference: Matthew 8:23–27

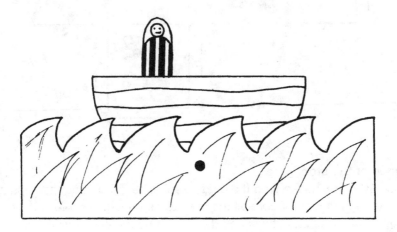

Each child will need
- a semi-circle of card approximately 15cm in diameter
- a piece of blue card approximately 25cm × 7cm
- a piece of card approximately 5cm × 2cm, rounded at one end
- a paper-fastener
- scissors, glue or sticky tape and felt pens

In advance of the story time

Use a blue pen to draw waves on the blue card. Draw wave peaks along one long side of the card and cut them out. Decorate the semi-circle of card to look like a boat. On the smaller piece of card draw a simple figure representing Jesus, colour in the figure and stick it so that he is standing in the boat. Attach the boat to the sea using a paper-fastener.

As the story is told

The boat can be rocked to and fro as the storm rages in the story.

DISCIPLES—FRIENDS OF JESUS

Bible reference: Matthew 10:1–4

This craft may be part of a review session after a series of lessons on the calling of the disciples, or it may be part of a lesson that looks at how Jesus had special friends with whom he worked.

Each child will need
- 2 strips of paper 30cm × 8cm
- scissors, sticky tape and felt pens

Fold each strip of paper concertina-wise into six sections.

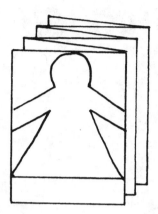

Draw a simple figure outline on the front of one folded strip, with the arms reaching to each edge of the section, plus a rectangle 1.5cm deep across the bottom of the section. Cut carefully through all six layers. Draw round the outline onto the other folded strip and again cut through all the layers. Join the two strips with sticky tape at an arm and at the base to form one long strip twelve disciples long. Colour them in and write the name of each in the boxes.

A MAN THROUGH THE ROOF

Bible reference: Mark 2:1–12

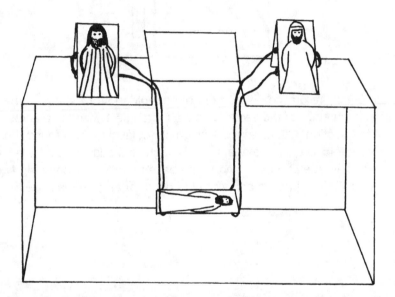

Each child will need
- a shoe-box or similar
- 3 pieces of card: two 12cm × 3cm, the third 6cm × 3cm
- a drinking straw cut to provide four 3cm lengths
- string—two lengths, each twice the width of the box plus 15cm
- scissors, sticky tape, reusable adhesive putty and felt pens

In advance of the story time

Turn the box on a long side and cut a flap in the centre of the 'roof' by making two slits 4cm deep and 7cm apart. Fold open the flap. Take the two longer pieces of card and fold them in half widthways. Draw a figure on either side of each so that the heads are up by the folds. Stick the four lengths of straw onto the back of the figures, 2cm up from each of their bases.

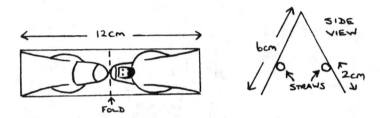

On the third piece of card draw a man (this is the paralysed man lying on his bed). Thread a length of string through one of the straws and back through the other straw on the same folded figure. With reusable adhesive putty, fix the ends of the string under either side of the head end of the paralysed man. Do the same with the second piece of string, using the other folded figure, this time attaching it to the feet end of the paralysed man.

As the story is told

Stand the two pairs of men on top of the 'roof' of the house, as far away from the opening as possible, with the man on his 'mat' between them and the flap in the roof closed. At the appropriate point in the story, open the flap and, moving the two pairs of men closer to the flap, lower the paralysed man through the hole to the ground. Remove the string and use the reusable adhesive putty to form a stand to stick the card into, allowing the paralysed man to stand.

GLOVE PUPPET DONKEY (PALM SUNDAY)

Bible reference: Mark 11:1–11

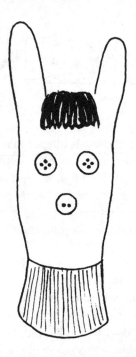

Each child will need
- a glove (for realism you will need grey or brown gloves but you may use any colour)
- wool and 3 buttons
- glue or a needle and thread

In advance of the story time
Turn inside the middle two fingers and the thumb of the glove (the two outer fingers form the ears of the donkey). Stick or stitch the thumb hole. Cut lengths of wool, or loop one length of wool, to form the fringe of the mane between the two ears. Stick or stitch in place. Choose two matching buttons for the eyes and another button for the nose. Stick or stitch in position.

As the story is told
Have the children put their puppets on when the donkey is collected by the disciples. They can play out the donkey passing through the shouting crowds.

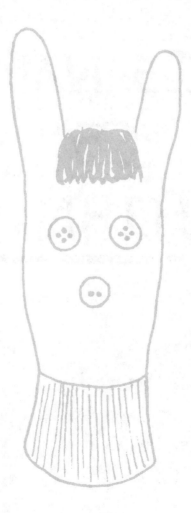

ZECHARIAH'S TABLET

Bible reference: Luke 1

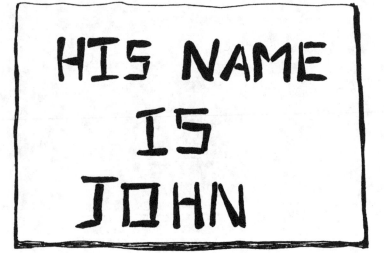

Each child will need
- plasticine or modelling dough (for a recipe see craft no. 55)
- a craft stick
- a plastic knife
- optional: a small rolling pin

In advance of the story time
Roll out, or pat flat, a lump of plasticine or modelling dough. Using a plastic knife, cut it to a rectangular shape approximately 12cm × 8cm.

At the end of the story
Use the craft stick to write on the tablet 'His name is John'.

THE TRANSFIGURATION

Bible reference: Luke 9:28–36

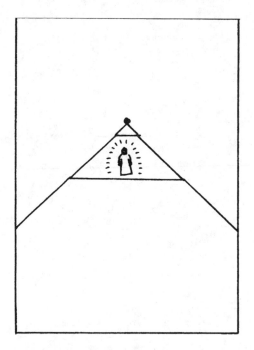

Each child will need
- an A4 sheet of blue card
- a square of green paper 21sq. cm
- a circle of card approximately 15cm in diameter
- a paper-fastener
- scissors, a ruler, glue and felt pens

As the story is told

Divide the circle into four quadrants. Position the square of green paper diagonally over the card so that one corner forms a mountain peak as high as possible without revealing the bottom corners of the card.

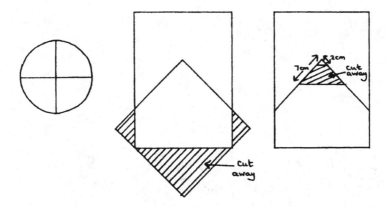

Trim the paper to fit the card and mark where the mountain peak is on the card. Remove the paper and cut off the top triangle with sides 7cm. Stick the remaining shape onto the card. Take the triangle and cut off the top triangle again, this time with sides 2cm. Stick this in position using the mark made for the mountain peak as a guide. Cut away the card from the revealed segment of the mountain. Use the paper-fastener to fix the circle behind the mountain so that its centre is behind the peak.

As the story is told

Stop at four points in the story for the children to draw in the quadrants revealed in the mountainside. In the first quadrant draw Jesus, Peter, John and James. Turn the circle from behind, and in the second quadrant draw Jesus shining brightly. In the third quadrant draw Moses, Elijah and Jesus, and in the fourth quadrant draw clouds. At the end of the story the children can return to the picture in the first quadrant.

TEN LEPERS CONCERTINA

Bible reference: Luke 17:11–19

Each child will need
- a strip of paper 50cm × 8cm
- scissors and felt pens

In advance of the story time

Fold the paper strip concertina-wise into ten sections. Draw a figure on the front section with the arms touching the edges. Write 'Thank you' on his robe. Carefully cut through all the layers. Unfold to reveal ten figures holding hands. On the side where the first figure has 'Thank you' on his robe, give each figure a happy face. Turn over and, on the reverse, give each figure an unhappy face.

STORY CRAFTS

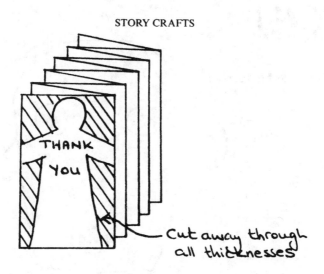

Cut away through all thicknesses

As the story is told

At the start of the story have the unhappy faces uppermost. When they are healed, turn the strip over to show that all the men were happy. To demonstrate how many returned to say 'thank you', fold them back into the concertina just showing the front figure again.

SOCK PUPPET SHEEP (THE SHEPHERD AND HIS FLOCK)

Bible reference: John 10:1–21

Each child will need
- a white sock
- a pink felt circle 4cm in diameter
- 2 white felt ovals 6cm × 3cm
- 3 buttons
- glue or a needle and thread, and a pen

In advance of the story time

Pull the sock over the hand so that the heel is over the knuckles. Turn the toe inside so that the fingers fit comfortably above and the thumb below this turned-in section. Mark where the ears and eyes should be with a pen and take the sock off the hand, keeping the required section turned in. Either stick or stitch the pink felt approximately 3cm inside, and to both the top and bottom, of the turned-in section so that a mouth is formed. Stick or stitch the white felt down each side of the head where marked, to represent the ears. Stick or stitch two matching buttons as the eyes where marked and the third button as the nose just above the mouth.

As the story is told

Have the children use the puppets throughout the story time. Ask them how the sheep felt towards their shepherd and how that helps them to understand their relationship with Jesus.

ROAD TO DAMASCUS COLOUR WHEEL

Bible reference: Acts 9:1–19

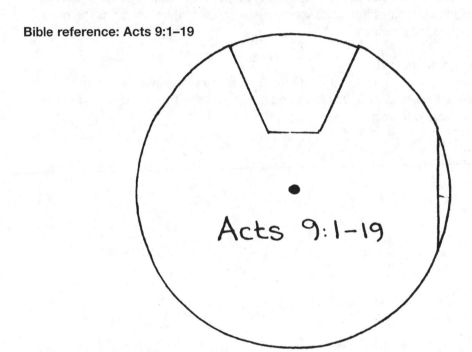

Acts 9:1-19

Each child will need
- 2 circles of card approximately 14cm in diameter
- coloured paper—red, yellow, black, blue and brightly multicoloured
- a paper-fastener
- scissors, a ruler, glue and felt pens

In advance of the story time

Divide one circle into six segments (the distance across the top of the segment will equal half the diameter). Cut the coloured paper to fit the segments and stick them in the following order: red, yellow, black, black, multicoloured and blue.

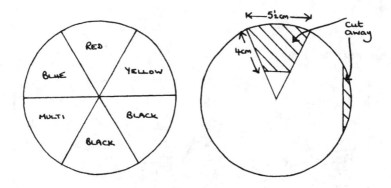

Find and mark the centre of the second circle. Mark a point on the circumference, and measure and mark 5.5cm across the circumference from the first point. From each of those points in turn, place the ruler joining them to the centre of the circle and draw a line 4cm down from the edge. Draw a third line joining the ends of the two lines. Now cut out this section. With the cutout section pointing upwards, cut a narrow slice off the right-hand side of the circle (left-hand side for left-handed children). Place the first circle behind the second and fix the two together using a paper-fastener through the centre of the circles. Write the Bible story reference on the front.

As the story is told

Turn the wheel to reveal the colours—red (Saul wanted to persecute and kill the Christians), yellow (the light from heaven), black (Saul is blinded and can no longer see), black again (to show that Saul remained blind for three days), bright colours (Saul could see again) and blue (Saul was baptised in water).

PAUL'S JOURNEYS BOARD GAME

Bible reference: Acts 13–28

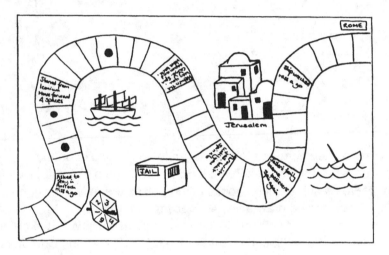

This is a craft that is ideally suited for a review lesson after a series of lessons learning about Paul's journeys.

Each child will need

- an A3 or larger sheet of paper
- a piece of card and a spent matchstick to make a spinner or a die
  (To make a spinner cut a hexagon, approximately 6cm across, out of the card. In each of the six segments write the numbers 1 to 6. Make a hole in the centre of the hexagon and push through the matchstick.)
- counters or discs of different coloured card
- felt pens

Design a board game that takes Paul on his journeys. Draw a track that loops around the board and devise advantage and forfeit squares. Decorate between the track with areas of sea, towns such as Jerusalem and Rome, and some of the people Paul encountered. The advantage and forfeit squares will depend on the stories studied but they could include: 'Asked to stay in Antioch to preach again next week. Miss a go', 'Stoned out of Iconium, fled to Lystra. Move forward double the number of squares shown on the spinner', 'Returned the way you came. Move back the number of squares shown on the spinner', 'Thrown into prison. Wait until you spin a 6', 'Jailer and family become believers. Spin again'.

To play the game
In groups of three or four, take it in turns to spin the spinner and move forward that number of squares, following the advantage or forfeit instructions on the square landed on. The winner is the first player to travel to the end of the track.

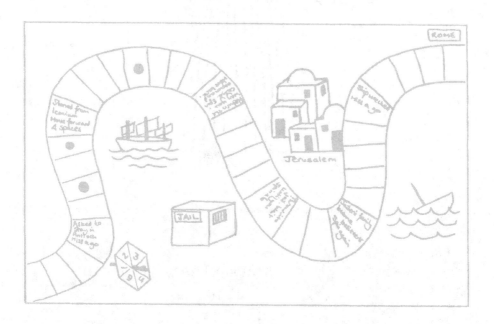

PAUL WAVES FAREWELL

Bible reference: Acts 20:13–38

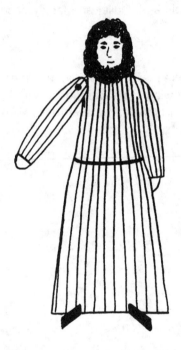

Each child will need
- a piece of card approximately 20cm × 12cm
- a paper-fastener
- scissors and felt pens

In advance of the story time

Draw the figure of Paul standing with his arms by his side on the card. Cut round the outline. Using a piece of the remaining card, cut out a second arm to match one of Paul's arms. Now cut away most of the corresponding arm from the figure of Paul, leaving the shoulder area so that the new arm can be fixed to the body with the paper-fastener. Colour both the main figure and the arm, and then join them together. Cut two slots 0.5cm deep in the base of the figure. Cut two strips of card 4cm × 1cm and cut a slot 0.5cm deep at the mid-point of each. Slot these strips into the base of Paul to enable him to stand.

As the story is told

The arm can be rotated as Paul says 'good-bye' to his friends.

Section Two:

LESSON REMINDER CRAFTS

These activities aim either to help children consider ways of applying a Bible lesson, or to act as a reminder of a Bible truth or verse.

Most of these crafts should be taken home, to act as a reminder of the lesson throughout the coming week, but the games (nos. 49 and 59) could be kept and used by the group over several weeks.

SPIRAL SNAKE

Bible reference: Genesis 3:1–13

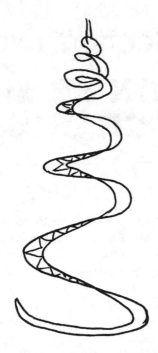

Each child will need
- a circle of card approximately 15cm in diameter
- cotton—approximately 30cm long
- scissors, felt pens and a needle

Draw a snake's head in the centre of the card and then draw a spiral out from the centre, keeping the lines 1–1.5cm apart. Write the Bible verse within the spiral, curling out from the centre, then decorate the rest of the snake. Carefully cut along the spiral line, trimming the end as a tail. Thread the cotton through the head of the snake and tie a knot to hold it in place.

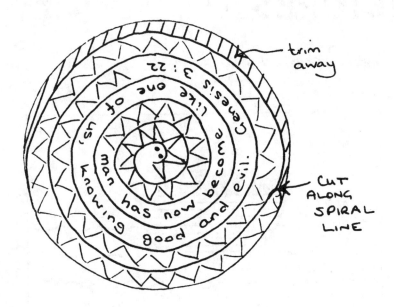

The snake will hang down from its head.

Bible verse: 'Man has now become like one of us, knowing good and evil' (Genesis 3:22).

RAINBOW REVERSE PICTURES

Bible reference: Genesis 7–9

Each child will need
- a sheet of paper, at least A4 in size
- various coloured wax crayons
- scissors, a ruler and a pencil

Use the ruler and pencil to divide the paper into two widthways. Thickly colour the entire top half of the paper with the wax crayons, so that it is covered with either stripes or small patches of different colours. Fold the bottom half of the paper up to cover the crayoned section.

FOLD

turn over
to reveal
rainbow
print

cut away
back

Pressing hard with the pencil, draw a picture—an animal, the ark, Noah, a dove or whatever you choose to act as a story reminder—shading the areas that you want to appear coloured. Unfold the paper to reveal your rainbow-coloured picture on the reverse. Cut away the half-sheet of paper covered in crayon.

RAINBOW AND DOVE MOBILE

Bible reference: Genesis 8:6–9:17

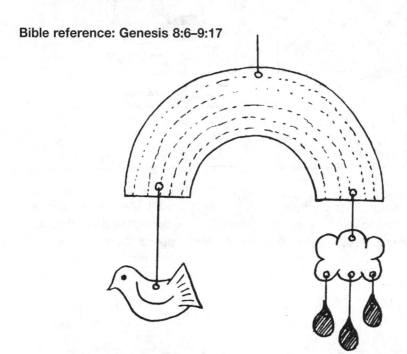

Each child will need
- an A4 sheet of white card
- cotton
- rainbow, cloud, raindrop and dove templates cut out of card
- scissors, felt pens and a hole-punch

Cut out a rainbow, a cloud, three raindrops and a dove.

On both sides of the card, colour the raindrops blue and the rainbow in stripes (from the top—red, orange, yellow, green, blue and purple). Punch holes at the

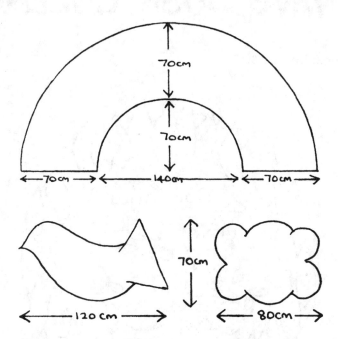

tops of all the pieces, at the bases of the rainbow and at three places along the base of the cloud. Thread cotton through the holes at the ends of the rainbow to suspend the dove and the cloud. Thread cotton through the hole at the top of each raindrop and attach them to the cloud. Finally thread cotton through the hole at the top of the rainbow to enable it to be hung up.

BURNING BUSH COLLAGE

Bible reference: Exodus 3:12

Each child will need
- a circle of card approximately 20cm in diameter
- yellow, orange and red paper
- glue and felt pens

Cut flame shapes, 3–4cm long, from the coloured paper and stick them all round the edge of the card circle, forming a border approximately 5cm wide. Write the Bible verse in the centre of the circle and then decorate the writing with leaves and branches.

Bible verse: 'God said, "I will be with you"' (Exodus 3:12).

BOX OF THE LAW

Bible reference: Exodus 40:20

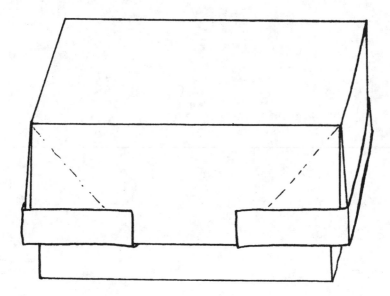

Each child will need
- a greetings card approximately 20cm × 15cm
- a piece of paper approximately 8cm × 5cm
- scissors, a ruler and felt pens

Select the greetings card bearing in mind that the centre of the picture on the card will form the lid of the box. Make the box in two halves—the lid from the front of the card and the base from the back of the card. So that the lid will fit over the base, cut 1cm off the top and one side of the back of the card. With the picture on the card face down, measure and draw the centre lines, dividing the card in half both ways. With the card lengthways, fold in from both edges to the centre line and open out again. With the card widthways, fold in from both edges to the centre fold. Then fold each of the four corners in to the crease-lines made by the lengthways folds.

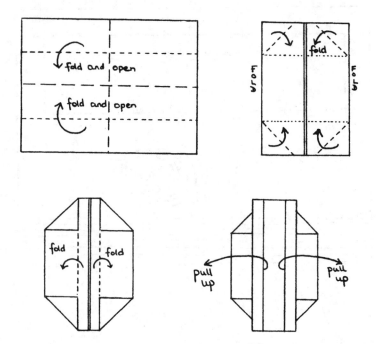

Fold back the edges over the corners. Hook your fingers under these flaps and gently pull up to form the sides of the box. Crease the corners into shape. Repeat for the base of the box.

Write the Ten Commandments or a key passage such as the one below on the piece of paper, roll it up and place it in the box.

Bible verses: 'The Lord, the Lord, the compassionate and gracious God, slow to anger, abounding in love and faithfulness, maintaining love to thousands, and forgiving wickedness, rebellion and sin' (Exodus 34:6–7).

WOOL COLLAGE

Bible reference: Judges 6:36–40

Each child will need
- an A3 or A4 sheet of stiff paper or card
- wool in various colours
- scissors, glue and felt pens

Design a picture from the story or a pattern using the wool cut into lengths and glued to the paper or card. Leave room to write the Bible verse in large letters somewhere on the collage.

Bible verse: 'The Lord accepts my prayer' (Psalm 6:9).

HEART REMINDERS

Bible reference: Ruth 1

Each child will need
- 6 red paper squares approximately 10sq. cm
- a strip of red or pink crêpe paper 75cm × 3cm
- a heart-shaped template cut from a piece of card 10sq. cm
- a stapler and felt pens

Draw round the heart template on each square of paper and cut out six hearts. On the first write the Bible verse and on the second write, 'I can show my love for God by. . . .' Then ask the children to think of four ways that they could show love to God by helping members of their family during the coming week. Write or draw each idea on the remaining four hearts. Staple the hearts on the strip of crêpe paper so that they hang downwards.

Bible verse: 'The Lord your God loves you' (Deuteronomy 23:5).

PRAYER-HOLDER

Bible reference: 1 Samuel 1

Each child will need
- 2 paper plates
- squares of paper that fit into the flat base of the plates
- a piece of string approximately 6cm
- scissors, sticky tape, a stapler and felt pens

Cut one plate in half. Place the rim of half a plate to the rim of the whole plate so that a pocket is formed between them. Staple them together around the rim. Decorate all round the rim of the holder and write the Bible verse in the centre of the half-plate at the front. Make a loop from the string and stick it to the back of the prayer-holder so that it can be hung up.

Encourage the children to write down prayers and to place them in their holder. Then they can periodically look through their prayer requests and see how God has answered. (Remember to review this with them every week or so and ask them to share some of the prayers that God has answered.)

Bible verse: 'In everything, by prayer and petition, with thanksgiving, present your requests to God' (Philippians 4:6).

RAFT OF LOGS

Bible reference: 1 Kings 5

help my sister to revise
tidy my bedroom
lay the table
hang out the washing
walk the dog
empty the dishwasher
read my sister a story
wash the car

Each child will need
- craft sticks
- glue and felt pens

You will need as many craft sticks as can be fitted side-by-side along the length of one stick, plus two extra sticks.

Keeping back the two extra sticks, have the children write a different idea about how they could be helpful to someone during the coming week along one side of each of the other sticks. Then, with the writing downwards, place the sticks side-by-side. Stick the two extra sticks across the back to fix them like a raft.

help my sister to revise

tidy my bedroom

lay the table

hang out the washing

walk the dog

empty the dishwasher

read my sister a story

wash the car

CLOCK

Bible reference: Proverbs 17:17

Each child will need
- a paper plate
- a piece of card 10cm × 8cm
- 2 pieces of card, 8cm × 1cm and 6cm × 1cm, pointed at one end
- a paper-fastener
- scissors, sticky tape or glue, and felt pens

Use the back of the plate as the clock face. Write the numbers one to twelve around the rim and the Bible verse on the clock face. Use the paper-fastener to fix the two strips of card to the centre of the plate, to form the clock hands.

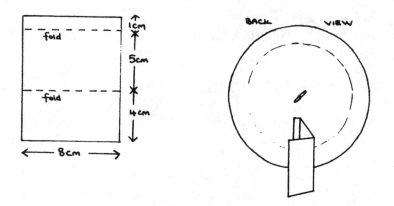

Fold the 10cm × 8cm piece of card into three as shown and stick the 1cm flap to the back of the clock from the six o'clock position up towards the centre. The clock will now stand upright.

Bible verse: 'A friend loves at all times' (Proverbs 17:17).

PRESSED-FLOWER BOOKMARK

Bible reference: Isaiah 40:8

Each child will need
- a piece of card 15cm × 5cm
- pressed flowers*
- clear, self-adhesive covering film
- scissors and felt pens

* Pressed flowers need to be prepared in advance. Pick small flowers when they are dry (not just after it has been raining or early in the morning). Lay a sheet of absorbent paper on a folded newspaper. Space out the flower heads on the paper, positioning them so that they are as flat as possible. Cover with another sheet of absorbent paper and some more newspaper. Place a heavy weight over the paper and leave them for a week. As an alternative to pressed flowers, you may use pictures of flowers cut from magazines or seed catalogues.

Write the Bible verse on the card and decorate the remaining space by carefully sticking on the pressed flowers. Cover the entire piece of card with clear self-adhesive covering film to keep the flowers from cracking off the card.

Bible verse: 'The grass withers and the flowers fall . . . but the word of our God stands for ever' (Isaiah 40:8).

SALT-SPRINKLED PICTURE

Bible reference: Matthew 5:13

Each child will need
- a large sheet of paper
- paints and a brush
- salt in a shaker

This project works best with fairly thick paint that doesn't dry immediately it's put on the paper, and a large brush. Paint a picture of a scene from Jesus' life, leaving a space at either the top or bottom of the paper to write the Bible verse. While the paint is still wet, sprinkle salt liberally over the entire picture and allow it to dry flat. When the painting is dry, pour off any excess salt. Where the salt has dried in the paint it will give it texture, and when it catches the light it will sparkle.

Older children may wish to be more selective when they sprinkle the salt on their picture, giving texture and sparkle to particular elements of their painting.

Bible verse: 'You are the salt of the earth' (Matthew 5:13).

CANDLE-LIGHT CONCERTINA

Bible reference: Matthew 5:14–16

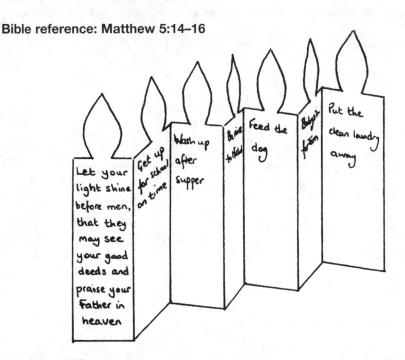

Each child will need
- a sheet of A4 paper
- scissors and felt pens

With the paper landscape fashion, fold it concertina-style into seven rectangles, each about 4.25cm wide.

With the paper still folded, draw a flame at the top of a candle. Cut round the flames and colour in the one at the front. Write the Bible verse on the front candle (for younger children you should have the verse printed for them to stick on and decorate). Unfold the candles.

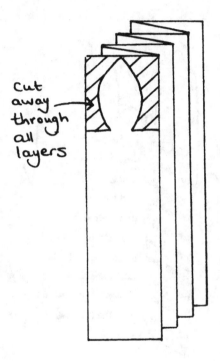

Cut away through all layers

Help the children to think of possible 'good things' that they could do during the coming week and have them write or draw six ideas, one on each candle. Encourage them to colour in each flame after they accomplish the 'good thing'.

Bible verse: 'Let your light shine before men, that they may see your good deeds and praise your Father in heaven' (Matthew 5:16).

PRAYING HANDS

Bible reference: Matthew 6:5–15

Each child will need
- a sheet of A4 paper
- scissors, felt pens and a pencil

Fold the paper in half widthways. Place your hand flat on the paper with the fingers closed and the little finger against the fold. Draw round the hand with the pencil. Cut round the hand outline, through both halves of the paper, leaving it joined at the fold.

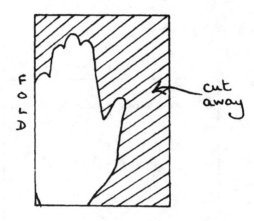

Write 'Matthew 6:5–15' on the outside. On the inside, with the hands opened out, copy the prayer from Matthew 6:9–13 or write the translation of the Lord's Prayer used in your church.

GROWING LILY

Bible reference: Matthew 6:25–34

Each child will need
- an A4 sheet of white paper
- an A4 sheet of green paper
- a piece of the same green paper approximately 30cm × 10cm
- scissors, glue and felt pens

Cut a 1cm strip off the top of both A4 sheets of paper. Draw the stem of a lily, 1cm wide and 15cm long going up from the centre of the bottom of the green sheet. Draw a leaf coming out from each side of the stem and then draw a three-petalled lily at the top of the stem approximately 9cm high, keeping the flower and the leaves within a 10cm strip down the centre of the paper. Cut out the lily, its stem and leaves. Place the green paper over the white paper and transfer the outline of the stem and leaves onto the white paper. Colour them in a different green to the paper. Cut a shallow arc at the bottom of the green paper strip, from one side to the other and approximately 2.5cm deep.

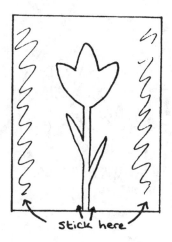
stick here

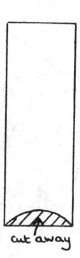
cut away

Replace the green sheet over the white sheet and stick the sheets together for a 4cm strip down both sides and just where the stem comes to the bottom of the paper. Write the Bible verse at the top of the green sheet, above the lily cut-out. Slide the strip of green paper, arc first from the top, in between the two sheets.

As you gently pull the green strip upwards the lily will grow, with leaves and then petals appearing.

Bible verse: 'Do not worry about tomorrow' (Mt 6:34).

PAINTED STONE

Bible reference: Matthew 7:24–27

Each child will need
- smooth stones approximately 5–8cm round
- enamel or acrylic paints
- PVA glue
- a paint brush

Paint a simple picture of a house on the stone and leave it to dry. If the stone is large enough, use a thin brush and add the Bible reference for the story. Alternatively, when the picture is dry, turn the stone over and paint the Bible reference on the base of the stone. Paint PVA glue over the picture. It will dry to give a shine like varnish.

COLLAGE COCKEREL

Bible reference: Matthew 26

Each child will need
- a square of card approximately 20sq. cm
- red, orange and yellow coloured paper
- a cockerel template (see page 223)
- scissors, glue and a thick black felt pen

Draw round the template onto the card and cut out the cockerel. Following the line where the wing would fold against the body, write the words 'Jesus is Lord'. Cut out feather shapes from the coloured paper and stick them onto the body of the cockerel, keeping the line of writing clear.

MAP COLLAGE

Bible reference: Matthew 28:19

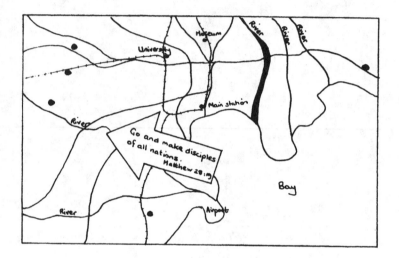

Each child will need
- a page from an old road or world atlas*
- a piece of paper approximately 10cm × 6cm
- scissors, glue and felt pens

* Road atlases seem to date so quickly that anyone who has to do much travelling regularly needs a new one. If you haven't got an old atlas at home I am sure that someone in your church will be able to let you have one. Alternatively, you may have access to computer software that will print off a map.

Carefully cut or tear out a page from the atlas and tidy up any torn edges with the scissors. Draw a broad arrow outline on the piece of paper and write the Bible verse inside the arrow. Cut out and stick the arrow, in any direction you wish, in the centre of the map.

Bible verse: 'Go and make disciples of all nations' (Matthew 28:19).

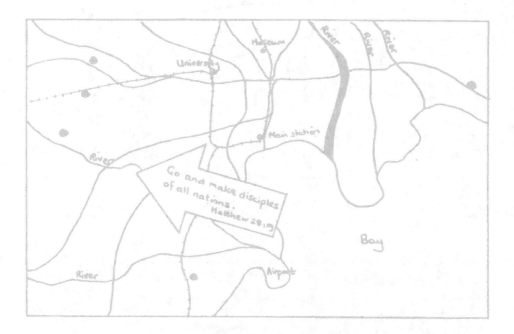

MAGNETIC FISH STORY REMINDER GAME

Bible reference: Luke 5:1–11

Each child will need
- 2 pieces of coloured paper approximately 12cm × 9cm
- 2 paper-clips
- scissors and felt pens

The group will also need a 'fishing rod' made from a magnet attached to a rod by string.

Draw a fish outline on each piece of paper. Draw in features such as an eye, scales, fins and tail and then cut out the fish. Slide a paper-clip onto the paper where the mouth would be. On the reverse of the fish draw a picture that represents a Bible story about Jesus that has been studied by the group recently (you will need to check that the picture will enable the others in the group to identify the story without ambiguity).

To play the game
All the fish need to be heaped together in a pile on the floor. The aim is to use the rod to catch a fish other than your own and identify the story from the picture. The children take it in turns to catch a fish. If they catch one of their own fish it must be thrown back. If they cannot correctly identify the story it must also be thrown back. If they do correctly identify the story they keep the fish. The winner is the player with the largest 'catch' at the end of the game.

ROAD SIGN

Bible reference: Luke 6:17–49

Each child will need
- a square of card approximately 10sq. cm
- a craft stick
- plasticine or reusable adhesive putty
- scissors, a ruler, sticky tape and felt pens

Choose whether to make a circular or triangular road sign. Cut out either a 10cm diameter circle or a triangle with a 10cm base and 8cm high. Colour a 1cm wide red border around the sign and write the Bible verse inside the border in black pen. Divide the craft stick into 1cm sections down its length and colour alternate sections black. Tape the stick to the back of the sign to act as the pole, and stand it up using the lump of plasticine or reusable adhesive putty.

Bible verse: 'I will instruct you and teach you in the way you should go' (Psalm 32:8).

MARY AND MARTHA STORY-WHEEL

Bible reference: Luke 10:38–42

Each child will need
- 2 circles of card approximately 14cm in diameter
- pictures from magazines or shopping catalogues
- a paper-fastener
- scissors, a ruler, glue and felt pens

Divide one circle into six segments (the distance across the top of the segment will equal half the diameter). Do the same to the back of the second circle. Measure down 4cm from the edge of each segment line for a pair of opposite segments on the second circle. Join up these points, and cut away the two sections.

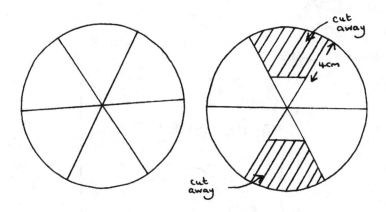

Place the first circle behind the second and fix the two together using a paper-fastener through the centre of the circles. With the cut-outs at the top and bottom, write 'MARY' under the top cut-out, 'MARTHA' above the bottom cut-out and 'Learn from the Lord' across the centre of the circle.

Using only pictures that are small enough to fit into the 5cm × 4cm revealed spaces, select three pictures that represent a modern-day Martha (for example, you may choose a vacuum cleaner, an iron and an oven) and three pictures that represent a modern-day Mary (for example, you may choose a book, a sofa and a CD player—to listen to the latest worship music or a recorded sermon). Cut out the pictures and stick one of Mary's pictures in the top space and one of Martha's in the bottom space. Turn the back circle through two segments and again stick one of Mary's pictures in the top space and one of Martha's in the bottom space. Turn the back circle through a further two segments and repeat with the final two pictures.

LOST SHEEP—WANTED POSTER

Bible reference: Luke 15:1–7

Each child will need
- an A3 sheet of paper
- cotton wool
- glue, a ruler and a black felt pen

Draw a 25cm square in the centre of the sheet of paper, leaving a border of just over 2cm on either side and 8cm at the top and bottom. Fill the square with an outline of a sheep's head. Draw in the features and stick on balls of the cotton wool to look like the sheep's fleece. In large letters write above the box 'LOST: ONE SHEEP' and below the box 'REWARD: REJOICING IN HEAVEN'.

'MY SPECIAL FRIEND JESUS' BADGE

Bible reference: John 1:35–51

Each child will need
- a circular self-adhesive label or a blank badge approximately 4–5cm in diameter
- felt pens

Encourage the children to think of a symbol that represents being a friend of Jesus—from the Bible reference they may think of a lamb (v.36) or a fish (Andrew and Simon were fishermen), but they may come up with other ideas of their own. Write 'MY SPECIAL FRIEND JESUS' around the edge of the label or badge and then draw the symbol inside. Either pin on the badge or peel the label off its backing and stick it on as a badge.

REVEALING A WAX PICTURE

Bible reference: John 3:19–21

I am the light of the world. John 8:12

Each child will need
- an A3 sheet of paper
- a white candle
- dark blue or black paint and a wide brush
- a ruler and a pen

Draw a line across the paper approximately 4cm up from the bottom. With the candle, and pressing quite hard, draw a simple picture of a candle, its flame and rays of light above the line (you will hardly be able to see anything on the paper). Using fairly thin black or dark blue paint and a wide brush, paint over the whole page, except for the bottom strip, revealing the wax picture. When the picture is dry, write the Bible verse along the bottom strip.

Bible verse: 'I am the light of the world' (John 8:12).

DOUGH-MAKING

Bible reference: John 6:25–59

This craft is the making of modelling dough. The dough is best if it stands for at least thirty minutes in the fridge or some other cool place after it is made and before it is used. The dough must not be eaten as it contains too much salt.

You could do this activity at the start of a session, have the story and review time and then finish the session by using the dough.

Alternatively you could make the dough at the end of the session for the children to play with at home (tell them to put it in the fridge for half an hour when they get home and warn parents to cover the table that the child uses for modelling).

Each child will need
- 1 cup of white flour
- 4 tablespoons of table salt
- 6 tablespoons of water
- 1 teaspoon of cooking oil
- food colouring
- a small polythene bag and bag-tie
- a mixing bowl and a spoon

Mix the flour and salt together and gradually add the water, stirring until the mixture is smooth. Knead the dough for about five minutes. Add a few drops of food colouring to the dough and continue to knead for at least another five minutes. Form the dough into a ball, put it into a polythene bag and seal the end with a bag-tie. Stand it in the fridge or some other cool place for thirty to sixty minutes before using it for modelling. Cover the work surface that the children use as the food colouring may stain table-tops.

If you have a range of food colourings, let the children make different coloured dough. When they come to use the dough, encourage them to share so that they can make models using a variety of colours.

If you don't have sufficient time or access to a fridge, make the dough at the end of the session and let the children take it home.

HELPFUL HANDS

Bible reference: Acts 9:32–43

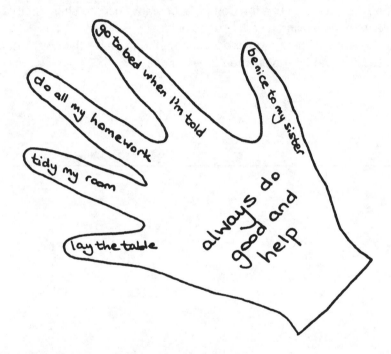

Each child will need
- a sheet of A4 paper
- scissors, felt pens and a pencil

Lay your hand flat in the middle of the sheet of paper, with the fingers splayed. Draw round the hand with the pencil and then cut round the outline. Think of five different ways that you could be helpful at home, at school or at church in the coming week, and use the felt pens to write one idea down each finger and the thumb.

Write 'Always do good and help' in the palm.

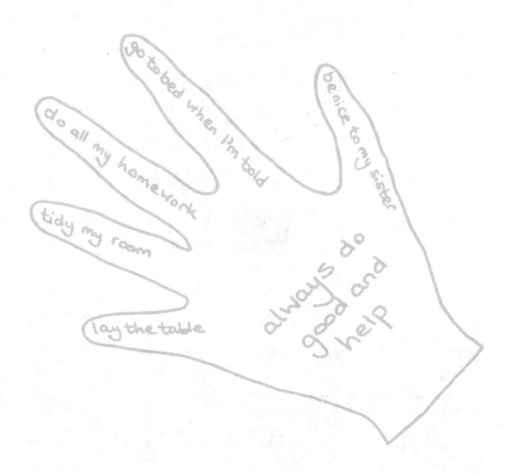

MONEY-BOX

Bible reference: 2 Corinthians 9:6–15

Each child will need
- a piece of card 27cm × 21cm
- pictures from magazines or catalogues
- scissors, glue and felt pens

Draw the net for the box on the card, score the lines to be folded and cut it out.

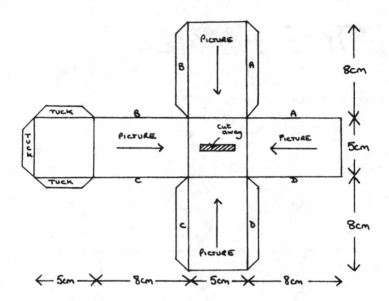

Choose pictures of needs supplied by God—e.g. food, clothes and homes. Cut them out and stick them to the four sides of the box as indicated on the template. Cut the slot in the top of the box. Make up the box by sticking the flaps A to D as indicated and tucking in the base flaps, so that the box can be opened. Write the Bible verse on the top of the box.

Bible verse: 'God loves a cheerful giver' (2 Corinthians 9:7).

LIFETIME MOBILE

Bible reference: 2 Timothy 1:3–7

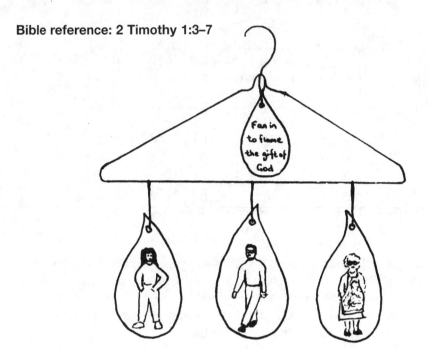

Each child will need
- a wire coat-hanger
- strips of orange crêpe paper 2cm wide
- 3 pieces of yellow card approximately 15cm × 9cm
- 1 piece of yellow card approximately 10cm × 6cm
- pictures from magazines or catalogues—two of children, two of parent-age adults and two of grandparent-age adults
- cotton
- scissors, glue, felt pens and a hole-punch

Wind the strips of crêpe paper round the coat-hanger until the wire is completely covered. Cut a flame shape out of each of the four pieces of yellow card. Stick the pictures on the three larger flames in pairs—the two children back and front of one flame, the two 'parents' back and front of another and the two 'grandparents' back and front of the third. On the smaller flame write the Bible verse on one side and the Bible reference for the verse on the other. Punch holes in the top of each flame. Cut a 10cm length of cotton, thread it through the hole in the smaller flame and tie the cotton round the top of the hanger so that the flame hangs within its framework. Cut three 20cm lengths of cotton and thread them through the other three flames, tying them along the lower wire of the hanger—one at each end and the third in the middle.

Bible verse: 'Fan into flame the gift of God' (2 Timothy 1:6).

BIBLE STORY PAIRS GAME

Luke 8:1-15

Luke 8:1-15

This is a craft activity that helps the group to revise the stories they have studied over the past few months.

Each child will need
- 4 squares of coloured card approximately 6sq. cm (All of the children's squares must be exactly the same size and colour. As an alternative you could give each child four cards from an old pack of playing cards with paper stuck over the card's value.)
- a Bible
- felt pens

Each child needs to think of a different Bible story that has been studied by the group over the past few months. The game will work best if the children don't know which stories have been chosen by the others in the group, so you will need to visit each in turn, making sure there is no duplication. On two of their cards they need to write the Bible reference for the story—encourage them to check in their Bible to be sure of being accurate. On the other two cards they should draw two representative scenes from the story (you will need to be the judge of whether the rest of the group will be able to identify the story from the two pictures).

To play the game
All the children's cards should be placed face down on the table and mixed around. The first player turns over two cards. They have a matching pair if they have the two pictures from a story, one picture and its Bible reference or two identical Bible references, but to win the cards they must be able to briefly tell the story. If they don't have a matching pair or they can't tell the story, they turn their cards back over. Play then moves to the person on their left. The winner is the player who has collected the most cards by the end of the game.

For younger children simplify the game by leaving out the Bible references, or by writing them underneath each picture.

BIBLE STORY CHOOSER

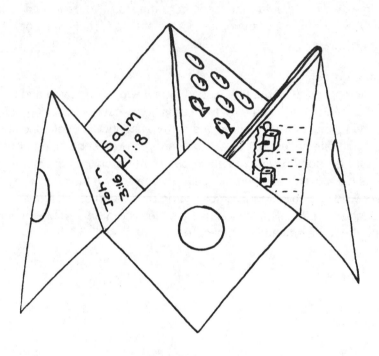

This craft can be used to review the stories and/or memory verses learned over the period of a month or a term.

Each child will need
- a square of paper approximately 20sq. cm
- felt pens

Fold the paper in half in both directions and open out. Fold each corner to the centre point. Turn this folded square over and again fold each corner to the centre point. Fold the resulting square in half one way, open and fold the other way.

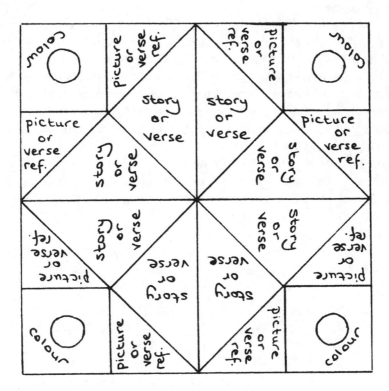

The chooser is used by putting the thumb and first finger of each hand into the four resulting flaps and easing the top corners to meet in the centre. The points are then moved apart in pairs, first the finger and thumb of each hand are pressed together and pulled away from each other, they are pushed together again so that all four points meet in the middle and then the two fingers and the two thumbs are pressed together and pulled away from each other. Before the chooser is played with, eight stories and/or memory verses need to be selected. Each of the four outer square flaps should have a different coloured circle drawn on it. Open the chooser so that the eight folded triangles lie flat. On each triangle, with the centre point downwards, either write the Bible reference of a memory verse or draw a simple picture that represents a Bible story. As each is written or drawn, lift up the triangle and write either the memory verse in full or a brief description of the story on the double triangle underneath. Re-form the chooser.

To play the game

In pairs, one operates their chooser while the other chooses and then they change over. The first choice is one of the four colours on the outer flaps. The operator then spells out the colour name (you may help them write this on the flap if they find spelling hard), opening the chooser in alternate directions on each letter. The next choice is one of the revealed Bible references or pictures. The chooser has to either recite the verse or briefly tell the story. The operator then opens the flap to confirm it is correct. If the game continues for several goes, the chooser always has to select a different verse or story.

You could make this into a team game, keeping scores. Each pair has one from each team and plays the game four times each. Points are awarded—one for each correctly retold story and two points for each correctly remembered verse.

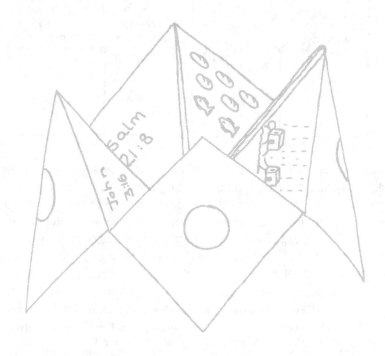

Section Three:
WORSHIP CRAFTS

These crafts may be used to help provide either a visual stimulus for, or a way of interacting with, times of worship.

Children often benefit from being able to visualise God's wonderful creation and many of these projects should be displayed in the worship area. The display may only be for a short time of worship at the end of the session when the craft is constructed, or it could be left up for a longer period, or possibly held over to be included in a service the following week.

In every case make sure that each child's work is clearly marked with their name and tell them when they will be able to have the craft to take home. Keep that commitment and ensure that projects which have been on display are carefully dismantled, showing that the child's handiwork has been honoured.

RAINBOW SILHOUETTE ANIMALS

Bible reference: Genesis 7:1–10

Each child will need
- an A5 sheet of card
- an A5 sheet of black paper
- different coloured wool
- 1 or 2 sequins
- scissors, glue and a pencil

Notch the two short edges of the card. Wind different coloured wool round the card in stripes so that it is completely covered in a thin layer, using the notches to keep it evenly distributed. Keep the wool fairly loose so that the card remains flat.

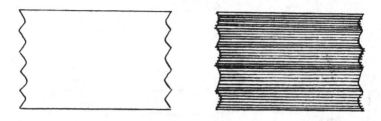

Draw an animal on the paper so that it covers most of the sheet but leaves a border of at least 2cm all round. Cut out the animal carefully, leaving the border intact. Stick the border onto the wool-covered card. Stick on the sequins as eyes.

Display the animals all round the room.

RAINBOW STREAMERS

Bible reference: Genesis 9:12–17

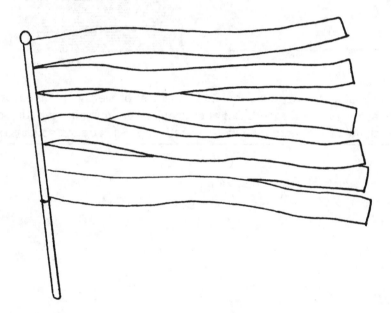

Each child will need
- crêpe paper strips 40cm × 3cm—one each in the six colours red, orange, yellow, green, blue and purple, plus an extra strip, in any colour, 20cm × 2cm
- a garden stick approximately 30cm long
- reusable adhesive putty or plasticine
- sticky tape

Stick one end of each of the six rainbow strips onto the seventh extra strip so that they are side by side and in the correct order for a rainbow. Cut 20cm of sticky tape and use it to stick the seventh strip along the garden stick so that the red strip is at the top. Use extra sticky tape to secure the strips at the top and bottom. Push a ball of reusable adhesive putty or plasticine firmly onto the top end of the stick to make it less dangerous when the children wave their streamers.

Let the children wave their streamers as part of their worship.

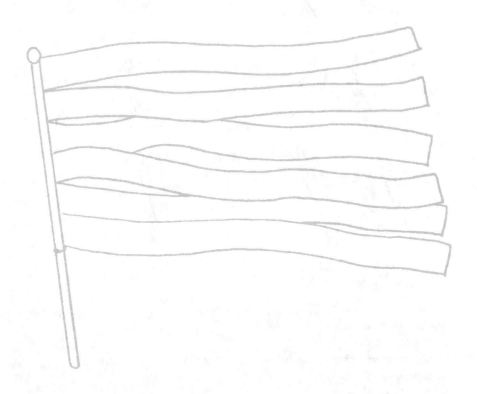

TAMBOURINE

Bible reference: Exodus 15:20

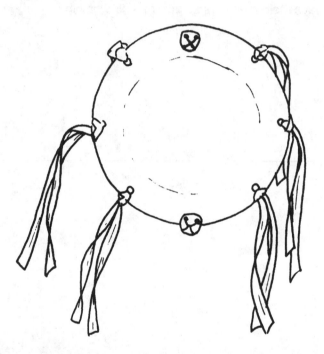

Each child will need
- a paper plate
- 8 coloured ribbons or crêpe paper strips 1–2cm wide and about 50cm long
- a hole-punch
- optional: two of the ribbons may be replaced with two bells, two bag-ties to attach them and sticky tape

Use the hole-punch to make eight holes equidistant around the rim of the plate. If you are using bells, thread the bag-ties through two opposite holes and use them to attach the bells firmly (use sticky tape to fix the ends of the ties to the plate). Fold a ribbon in half lengthways and thread the folded end through a hole, then pass the two ends through the loop that is formed and pull tight. Repeat with the remaining ribbons.

These tambourines will provide a fairly quiet accompaniment to songs!

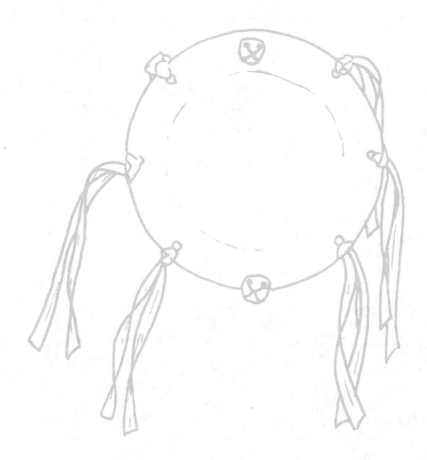

TABERNACLE BANNERS

Bible reference: Exodus 26:1

Each child will need
- blue, red or purple cotton material triangles, 20cm across the top and 30cm from the centre of the top to the point
- a paper triangle 20cm across the top and 28cm from the centre of the top to the point
- blue, red and purple fabric paint
- a pencil, a needle and thread or glue that will stick fabric

Note: These will look particularly effective if you have an equal number of triangles in the three different colours of fabric.

Draw a simple design of cherubim on the paper triangle. Turn down 2cm along the top of the material triangle and either stitch or stick, leaving a pocket through which a cord can be threaded. Read the instructions for the particular fabric paints that you have and, following them carefully, copy the paper design onto the material. If necessary fix the paint with an iron (have an adult do this).

The triangular pendants can be strung onto thick string or cord—red, blue and purple alternately if possible—and hung around the worship area.

BUTTERFLY

Bible reference: 1 Samuel 10:6

Each child will need
- an A4 sheet of coloured tissue paper
- a paper-covered bag-tie
- scraps of other coloured tissue paper or glitter or sequins
- scissors and glue

Fold the tissue paper in half lengthways and cut rounded corners at each end of the fold. Twist the bag-tie tightly round the centre of the folded paper, open out the wings and form the ends of the bag-tie into antennae.

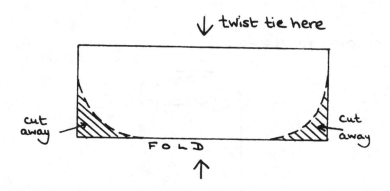

Decorate the wings with scraps of other coloured tissue paper or glitter or sequins.

The butterflies can be displayed around the worship area or you may stick straws to the body so that the children can hold them.

──────────────── TIP ────────────────
Glue sticks are easier for young children to use than PVA glue. They are also less wasteful and a lot less messy to clear away!
──

SHAKERS

Bible reference: 2 Samuel 6:1–5

Each child will need

- a sealable tube (any size, from a film tube to a sweet or crisp tube)
- a small handful of grains of rice
- paper to cover the outside of the tube
- scissors, glue, masking tape and felt pens

Cut the paper the exact length of the tube and the correct width to wrap round the tube with a 1cm overlap. Decorate the paper, including the words 'Celebrate with all your might before the Lord'. Wrap the paper round the tube, sticking down the overlap. Pour the grains of rice into the tube. Use the masking tape to stick the ends of the paper down, sealing the top and bottom of the tube at the same time so the rice cannot fall out.

The children can use their shakers to join in with the music.

SOLOMON'S TEMPLE DESIGNS

Bible reference: 1 Kings 6:29–35

Each child will need
- A2 sheet of light brown card or paper
- a pencil and a black marker, or thick felt pen

Look at the descriptions of the temple panels in the Bible. Using a pencil draw designs of cherubim, palm trees and flowers on the brown card or paper. When you are happy with the design go over it in black pen.

Display the panels on the walls in the worship area.

PRAYER WALL

Bible reference: Nehemiah 1:1–2:18

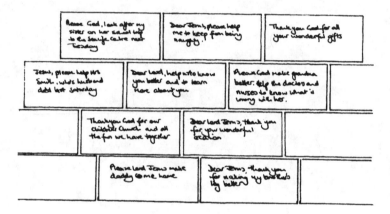

This is a group project to be completed over two or more weeks. The aim is to build a wall through prayer.

Each child will need
- several squares of grey or brown card approximately 19sq. cm
- scissors, glue and a pen

Draw the net of a brick on a square of card, score the lines to be folded and cut it out. Write a prayer on the side of the brick, as shown on the net. Make up the brick by sticking the flaps in the order indicated (A to G). Have the children start to build a wall two or three bricks high. They should take the remaining squares of card home. Throughout the week they should write down their prayers on the bricks, make them up and bring them back the following week. They can add them to the wall started the previous week.

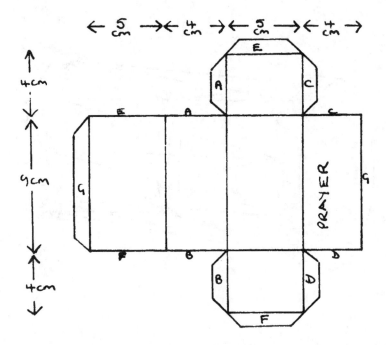

You may set a limit to the height of the wall and see how long it takes to reach, or you may see how high you can build the wall in two, three or four weeks. At the end of the activity review the prayers and see how many have been answered.

As an alternative, you could use a selection of large boxes, from shoe-boxes to supermarket boxes. The children could then write their prayers on sheets of paper which they stick onto the side of their box to build a wall that won't topple.

TOM-TOM DRUM

Bible reference: Psalm 150

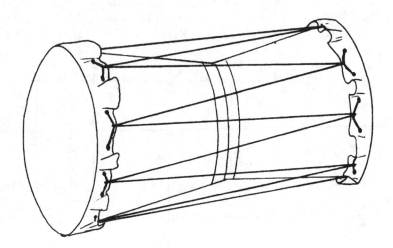

Each child will need

- 2 plastic flowerpots approximately 8cm in diameter
- 2 circles of cotton material approximately 14cm in diameter
- thin string
- masking tape, PVA glue, a paint brush and a large-eyed needle

Using masking tape, stick the two flowerpots together base to base. Thread a large-eyed needle with approximately 40cm of string. Make large tacking stitches, about 2cm long, 2cm in from the edge of one of the material circles. Place the circle over one of the flowerpots and pull and tie the two ends of the string so that the material fits tightly over the opening. Repeat for the other circle. Cut a length of string about 150cm. Weave it through a string loop of one circle, down through a string loop on the other circle, back through the next loop on the first circle and so on all the way round. Pull the string as tight as possible and tie securely. Paint PVA glue over the flat surfaces of the material at either end of the drum to make it more effective.

If you have also made the tambourines (craft no. 63) and shakers (craft no. 66), let the children work out an accompaniment to a song of their choosing.

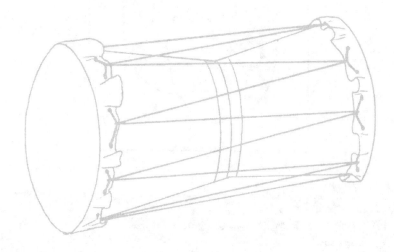

PRAISE BANNERS

Bible reference: Psalm 150

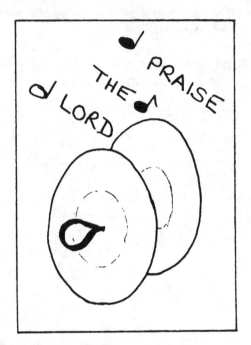

Each child will need
- an A2 or A3 sheet of brightly coloured paper
- marker pens

Note: It would be helpful to have a book containing pictures of musical instruments for the children to look through as they undertake this project.

Select an instrument mentioned in Psalm 150—trumpet, harp, lyre, tambourine, strings, flute or cymbals—and draw it as large as possible with marker pens onto a sheet of brightly coloured paper. Write 'PRAISE THE LORD' on the paper in an original way that suggests it is coming from the instrument.

Display the pictures around the worship area.

NAMES OF JESUS FLAGS

**Bible references: Isaiah 7:14; 9:6; 53:1; 59:20;
John 6:35; 9:5; 10:9; 10:11; 11:25; 15:1**

*Depending on the number of children participating in this activity, you
may use the Isaiah references, the John references or both.*

Each child will need
- a square of white cotton material approximately 40sq. cm (this is the
  size of a large handkerchief)
- a square of paper approximately 40 sq. cm
- fabric paints
- a garden cane approximately 50cm long
- reusable adhesive putty or plasticine
- a pencil and a staple gun

Use the paper square to work out a design that incorporates one of the names used to describe Jesus. Read the instructions for the particular fabric paints that you have and, following them carefully, copy the paper design onto the material. If necessary, fix the paint with an iron (have an adult do this). Use the staple gun to attach the square of material to the cane to form a flag with a short handle. Push a ball of reusable adhesive putty or plasticine firmly onto the top end of the stick to make it less dangerous (a short handle also helps make the flag safer when it is being waved).

Let the children wave their flags as part of their worship.

FLOWERS COLLAGE

Bible reference: Isaiah 40:6–8

Each child will need
- an A3 sheet of paper
- a white paper circle approximately 15cm in diameter
- pictures of flowers from magazines or catalogues
- scissors, glue and felt pens

Cut out a selection of pictures of flowers and stick them on the sheet of paper, covering it completely. Draw petal shapes around the edge of the paper circle and cut them out. Write the Bible verse in the centre and stick it onto the flower background.

The pictures can be displayed together as a large panel.

Bible verse: 'The word of our God stands for ever' (Isaiah 40:8).

———————————————————————— TIP ————————————————————————

Save magazines and catalogues for collage crafts. Seed catalogues are good for plants and flowers, clothing catalogues for people, supermarket magazines for food, nature magazines for animals and scenery. Periodically go through the pile you have collected and tear out the pages that have pictures that you think will be useful. Also tear out pages that have large blocks of colour or texture—you will often find these in the adverts and art pages in the weekend newspaper supplements. Keep the torn-out pages in a box file, or divide them between envelope folders by category. This reduces storage and makes finding appropriate pictures much easier.

GOD'S KINGDOM BALLOONS

Bible reference: Matthew 13:45–46

Each child will need
- a pearly or white balloon
- a circle of card approximately 20cm in diameter
- narrow paper curling ribbon
- felt pens and a hole-punch

Write 'Seek the kingdom of heaven' in large letters on the card and punch a hole through the card to the right-hand side of the text. Blow up the balloon. Before tying a knot, thread the card onto the neck of the balloon. Tie a knot and then tie a length of the ribbon onto the end of the balloon.

Let the children wave their balloons as part of their worship.

CHILDREN COLLAGE

Bible reference: Mark 10:13–16

This craft enables the children to work on their own section of a larger, composite display.

Each child will need

- an A4 sheet of card
- pictures of children from magazines or catalogues
- photographs of the children—taken either in advance, so they can have been developed beforehand, or with an instant photo camera
- a strip of paper approximately 8cm × 200cm (the length of this strip will depend on the number of children taking part in this activity and the size of the display area available)
- a self-adhesive label
- scissors, glue and felt pens

Cut out pictures of children of all ages and stick them onto the card, covering it completely. Each child should stick their own photograph somewhere on the card among all the other children. They should write their name onto the label and add it to the collage near to their photo.

One person may write the Bible verse onto the strip of paper, or the paper may be divided into sections for different people to write. All of the card collages should be grouped together, effectively forming a single display that includes all the children in your group, with the Bible verse running through the centre or along the bottom.

Bible verse: 'Let the little children come to me, and do not hinder them, for the kingdom of God belongs to such as these' (Mark 10:14).

PALM STREAMERS

Bible reference: Mark 11:1–11

Each child will need
- a tube from the inside of a kitchen towel roll
- 12–15 green crêpe paper strips approximately 2cm × 40cm
- scissors and sticky tape
- optional: brown paint and a brush

Optional: Paint the tube brown and leave it to dry.

Use sticky tape to stick one end of each strip of crêpe paper to the inside of the tube, ensuring that the strips are spread evenly all round one end of the tube.

Hold the tube and wave it to represent a palm branch.

CANDLE CURTAINS

Bible reference: Luke 2:8–20

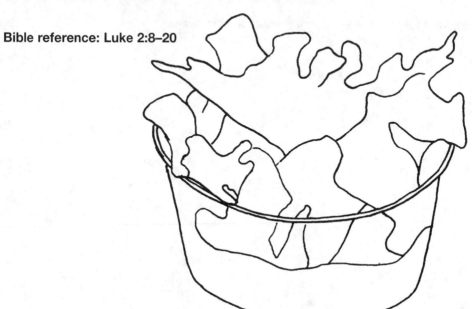

This craft would make a particularly interesting addition to any Christmas-time candle-lit service. As hot wax is used, it needs careful adult supervision.

Each child will need
- 2 or 3 candle ends (for each child these should all be either the same colour or white and one other colour, but if different children have a variety of colours it will make the finished effect more interesting)
- a night light
- a small metal foil or plastic dish (an individual pie dish or a plastic dish suitable for party jellies is about the right size)
- a small saucepan for melting the wax (a double saucepan is best, to avoid the wax overheating) and a heat source

In addition, everyone needs access to a bucket of cold water.

Gently melt the wax in the saucepan. Carefully pour it into the dish, filling it to between a quarter and a third full. Hold the rim of the dish with both hands and plunge it quickly deep into the bucket of water. Hot wax can be dangerous. Do not allow younger children to do this themselves. Older children must be carefully supervised. If any children are wary of the hot wax have an old pair of gloves that they can put on as they do this. The wax immediately cools and won't pass through even woollen gloves. The wax will solidify as it rises out of the dish, making an irregular curtain standing in the dish. The faster the dish is plunged into the bucket, the better the effect. If it does not work the first time, scrape the wax out of the dish, re-heat and try again. Place the night light in the dish (if there is not room for a night light you could use a short candle, but it will not last as long).

Stand the dish so that the light is seen through the curtain when it is lit.

HARVEST BANNER

Bible reference: Luke 10:1–2

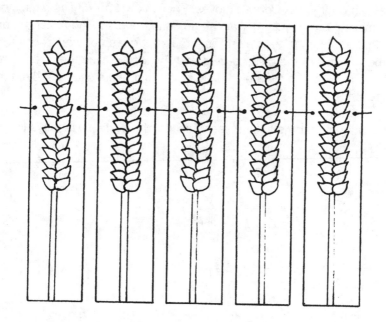

Each child will need
- a piece of light green card approximately 10cm × 50cm
- a strip of light brown paper 1.5cm × 25cm
- tissue paper in shades of yellow, orange and brown
- scissors, glue and a hole-punch

Stick the brown paper stem onto the card, going up from the centre of the base of the card. Cut out 'kernels' of corn from the different colours of tissue paper. These should be drop shapes approximately 3cm × 4cm and you will need an odd number—somewhere between twenty-nine and thirty-five. Stick one kernel pointing upwards on a line continuing up from the brown paper but almost at the top of the card. Then stick pairs of kernels, each pair overlapping the last, going down the card until approximately 5cm of the stem has been covered. Punch holes on either side of the card, approximately 15cm down from the top.

Thread a string of the stems of corn and, for best effect, display them at waist height away from a wall so that they will move in the air currents, looking like a field ready for harvest.

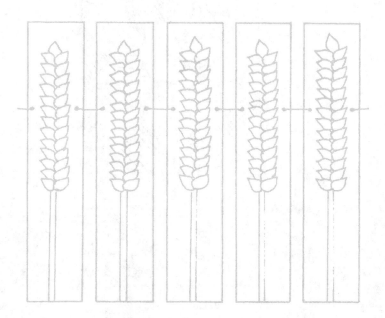

STAINED-GLASS CANDLE-HOLDER

Bible reference: John 8:12

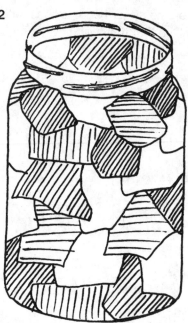

Each child will need
- a jam jar
- a night light
- scraps of tissue paper in several colours
- PVA glue and a brush

Stick torn scraps of tissue paper all over the outside of the jam jar (do not stick the paper inside the jar thinking it will look more effective—it could catch light). Brush glue all over the outside of the paper. This will give a shiny effect once it has dried and the paper won't start to lift off. Place a night light inside the jar and, when lit, it will give a stained-glass glow.

Place all the lights in a circle and gather round them for a time of worship.

Note: The jars will get very hot when the night lights are lit so do not attempt to move them until they have been allowed to cool down.

─────────────────── TIP ───────────────────
Collect up the tissue paper crowns from crackers after a party and you will have a range of colours!

PRAYERS BEHIND BARS

Bible reference: Acts 12:1–17

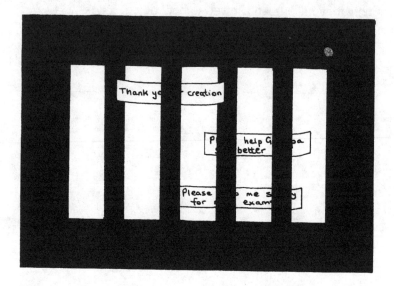

Each child will need
- an A4 sheet of card
- an A4 sheet of black paper
- several strips of paper 10–15cm × 2cm
- scissors, a ruler, glue, a pencil and felt pens

Leaving a 4cm border around the edge of the black paper, mark 'bars' 1.5cm wide and just over 3cm apart. Carefully cut away the remaining paper. Stick the paper onto the card by the borders only, so that the 'bars' are free to be lifted away from the card. Write prayers on the paper strips and weave them behind the 'bars'.

Display a group of prison cells on a board or around the room and invite the whole church to add their prayers.

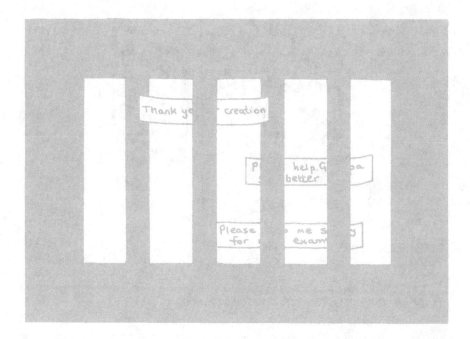

WORSHIP CUBE

A craft to help explore what 'worship' means.

Each child will need
- a piece of card 29cm × 23cm
- scissors, glue and felt pens

Draw the net of the cube onto the card (each side is 7cm and the flaps are 1cm wide) and cut it out. Score all the lines to be folded. Make up the cube by sticking all the flaps under the faces as marked and in the order indicated (A through to G). On five sides of the cube illustrate and/or write five of the elements that can contribute to worship: prayer, song, music, reading and listening. On the sixth side write 'WORSHIP'.

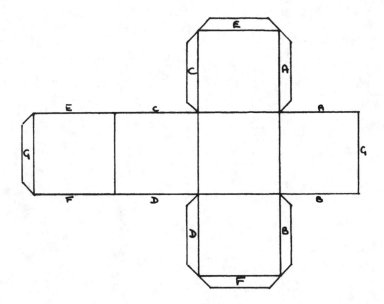

The cubes may be used to help children understand how your church time of worship is put together—stacking the cubes with the appropriate sides in order. Alternatively, the children could use them to plan their own time of worship.

Instead of making small boxes, the children could decorate large supermarket boxes which could be stacked at the front of the church one Sunday morning to give the children (and the adults) a visual representation of the order of service and show how it fits together as a coherent time of worship.

Section Four:
CRAFTS TO GIVE

These crafts provide children with opportunities to share lessons with their family or evangelise to their friends as they explain why they have made the items they are giving.

With simple crafts it is often appropriate to allow young children to make two—one to keep and one to give—as sharing rather than giving is an equally valid lesson for them to learn.

Several of the crafts that are in the other four sections are also appropriate for giving—especially those in the Seasonal section.

CREATION CALENDAR

Bible reference: Genesis 1

Each child will need
- a photocopy of each of the six sheets that make up the calendar*
- an A4 sheet of card
- a 10cm length of wool or a bought picture hanger
- scissors, sticky tape, glue, felt pens and a stapler
- optional: pictures cut from magazines

* The calendar sheets need to be prepared in advance. Divide a sheet of A4 paper in half and then divide the lower half into two widthways. Print a calendar for January in the left-hand half and a calendar for February in the right-hand half. Prepare five more sheets in a similar fashion for March/April, May/June, July/August, September/October and November/December.

Either draw pictures or find appropriate pictures to cut out of magazines for each of the six top halves of the calendar sheets:

- The January/February picture should show land, sea and sky.
- The March/April picture should show trees and plants.
- The May/June picture should show the sky with the sun or moon and stars.
- The July/August picture should show fish and birds.
- The September/October picture should show animals.
- The November/December picture should show people.

Staple the sheets to the card in the correct order, so that the card forms the back of the calendar, then stick the wool onto the reverse of the card to provide a hanger.

PLACE MATS

Bible reference: Exodus 16

This is an ideal gift for a younger brother, sister or friend.

Each child will need
- a piece of coloured card 40cm × 30cm
- a piece of contrasting coloured paper approximately 20cm × 8cm
- a square of white paper 22sq. cm
- pictures of food cut from magazines
- clear, self-adhesive covering film
- a plate, approximately 20–22cm in diameter, to draw round
- scissors, glue and felt pens

Place the plate upside down on the white square of paper, draw round it and cut it out. Stick the paper plate onto the card, so that the centre is 15cm from the right edge of the card, and then stick pictures of food all over the plate. Stick the paper rectangle to the left of the plate, as if it were a folded serviette and write the Bible verse on it. Decorate the remaining card as if it were a place mat. Cover the front and back of the card with the clear, self-adhesive film so that the place mat can be wiped clean.

Bible verse: 'Know that I am the Lord your God' (Exodus 16:12).

CLAY POTS

Bible reference: 2 Kings 4:1–7

This craft will take two weeks to complete.

Each child will need
- modelling material*
- a tube from the inside of a kitchen towel roll
- a cutting tool and a rolling pin
- varnish and a brush

* You may use clay for this craft (in which case you will need to paint the pots) but, unless you have access to a kiln, the pots cannot be fired. As an alternative there are many proprietary brands of modelling material available from craft shops or good stationers that come in a range of colours and won't need painting. Some dry at room temperature, others need baking in an oven. For this craft you will need at least two colours.

Follow the general instructions for the modelling material that you are using. Roll out the material about 0.5cm thick. Place the end of the tube on the material and cut out a circle that size, then cut out a rectangle 14cm × 6cm. Stand the tube over the circle, which forms the base of the pot, and wrap the rectangle round the tube to form the body. Join the pieces together, then remove the tube. Take a different coloured material and form or cut out shapes to stick on the outside of the pot as decoration.

   Leave to harden, or bake as instructed, and then varnish the following week.

'SPECIAL TO GOD' CERTIFICATES

Bible reference: Psalm 121:7–8

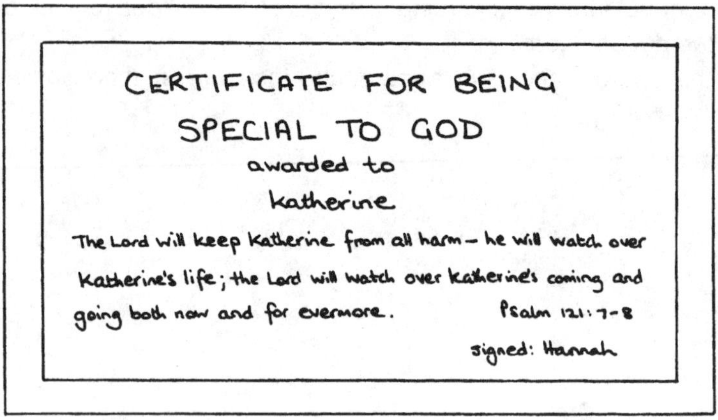

CERTIFICATE FOR BEING
SPECIAL TO GOD
awarded to
Katherine

The Lord will keep Katherine from all harm – he will watch over Katherine's life; the Lord will watch over Katherine's coming and going both now and for evermore. Psalm 121:7-8

signed: Hannah

Each child will need
- an A4 sheet of paper (several computer programs will generate borders or even certificate templates that you may wish to print out and photocopy)
- a black pen

If you have not provided a certificate background then a border needs to be drawn on the paper. Choose someone you would like to tell that they are special to God. Write 'CERTIFICATE FOR BEING SPECIAL TO GOD' at the top of the sheet and then 'AWARDED TO' followed by the chosen person's name. Copy the Bible verse underneath, replacing every *you* and *your* with the person's name. Finally, sign and date the certificate.

Bible verse: 'The Lord will keep *you* from all harm—he will watch over *your* life; the Lord will watch over *your* coming and going both now and for evermore' (Psalm 121:7–8).

CERTIFICATE FOR BEING
SPECIAL TO GOD
awarded to
Katherine

The Lord will keep Katherine from all harm — he will watch over Katherine's life; the Lord will watch over Katherine's coming and going both now and for evermore.   Psalm 121:7-8

signed: Hannah

CARPENTER'S GIFT

Bible reference: Luke 2

Pyrography is the craft of burning designs onto wood. It is possible to purchase a starter set, which will include a pyrography iron and basic instructions. Someone in your church, even one of the older children, may have one you could borrow. Close adult supervision is necessary as the iron gets very hot.

Each child will need
- a rectangle of wood or a plain wooden napkin ring
- a sheet of paper
- a pencil

Note: Have a spare piece of wood for everyone to practise on before they start their project.

Use the paper and pencil to work out a simple design—it could be just a name on the napkin ring or '[*name*]'s Room' plus a pattern on the rectangle. Draw the design onto the wood to act as a guide for the iron. Work on a heat resistant surface and follow the instructions that accompany the iron carefully. The iron will take a few minutes to heat up, then it is the length of time that the iron is in contact with the wood that determines the darkness of the line. The smoother you can move the iron on the wood the better the finished article will look.

STAINED-GLASS PICTURE

Bible reference: Luke 7:36–50

Each child will need
- an A4 sheet of white paper
- an A4 sheet of grey, or stone effect, paper
- baby oil or odourless vegetable oil
- a cotton wool ball
- wax crayons
- a ruler, glue, a pencil and a thick black pen

Draw a window outline on the grey paper and cut away the window area. Place the white paper underneath the grey and draw round the cut-out area, transferring the window outline onto the white paper. In the window area of the white paper draw a picture from the story. Divide the picture up to look like stained glass and go over all the outlines in thick black pen. If younger children will find this too difficult, provide them with a photocopied picture already outlined in black. Use wax crayons to colour in the picture inside the window, leaving some 'clear glass' areas uncoloured. Dip the cotton wool ball into the oil and wipe it all over the wax picture. This will make the window translucent. Stick the grey paper over the white, revealing the window in its stone surround.

Suggest that the picture is displayed in a window or in front of a light for best effect.

ENVELOPE BASKETS

Bible reference: John 6:1–15

Each child will need
- an envelope (the size and shape will determine the size and shape of the basket)
- scissors and felt pens

Seal the envelope and fold it in half lengthways. Draw the handle on the fold and cut it out.

Unfold the envelope and ease open the basket pouch. Decorate the basket as elaborately as you wish, adding a simple message such as 'God cares for you'.

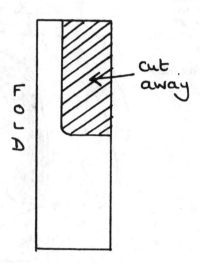

Ideas for gifts to place in the basket:

- line the basket with a small plastic bag for a posy of flowers
- sweets
- a posy of paper flowers
- a small packet of tissues

SALT DOUGH FRAMES

Bible reference: John 6:25–59

This craft will take two weeks to complete.

Each child will need
- either ready-prepared salt dough or the ingredients to make the dough*
- a small, heart-shaped biscuit cutter and a rolling pin
- a circle of card 11cm in diameter
- a circular picture 8cm in diameter—this may be a picture cut from a magazine or a picture of the child (you could take photographs of the children during the first session and have them developed to use during the second session)
- varnish and a brush
- strong glue

* Quantity for three frames: one cup of white flour, half a cup of table salt, a teaspoon of cocoa (for colouring) and half a cup of water. Mix the ingredients together, adding slightly more or less water to give a good dough consistency. Knead for ten to fifteen minutes and then cover and let the dough stand for at least thirty minutes before use. The dough must *not* be eaten as it contains too much salt.

Use about one third of the dough. Roll out a small piece of the dough quite thinly and cut out a heart shape. Divide the remaining dough into two equal pieces and gently form them into two long sausage shapes 1–2cm thick. Twist the two lengths together and form them into a circle around the inside edge of the circle of card. Cut off any excess, press the ends together to complete the circle and cover the join with the heart, using a little water to stick the dough in place. Gently transfer the frame onto a baking sheet. It will need six or seven hours in an oven at 100°C to dry out completely. Keep in a dry place until the following week.

Stick the picture into the centre of the card circle and then stick the dough frame down around the edge. Varnish the front of the frame.

'THE LORD CARES' CARD

Bible reference: John 14:15–21

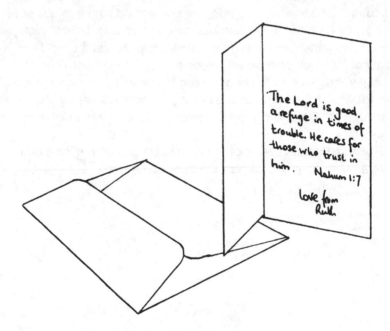

The Lord is good,
a refuge in times of
trouble. He cares for
those who trust in
him.   Nahum 1:7

love from
Ruth.

Each child will need
- an A5 sheet of card
- an envelope to fit the card
- pictures cut from old greetings cards or magazines
- scissors, glue and felt pens

Fold the card in half. Decide who you will make the card for—maybe there is someone you know who is unhappy or has a problem who might like to be reminded of how much God cares for them. Select a picture, or group of pictures, that will appeal to your chosen person. Cut them out, arrange and stick them onto the front of the card. Inside the card write the Bible verse.

Bible verse: 'The Lord is good, a refuge in times of trouble. He cares for those who trust in him' (Nahum 1:7).

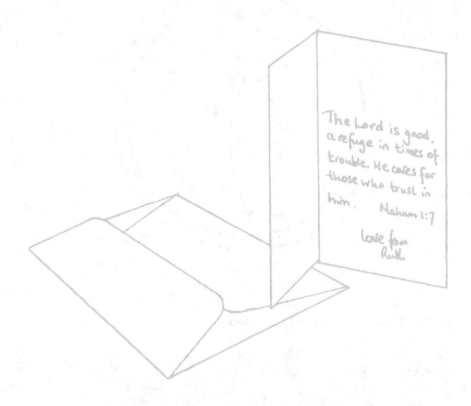

SPLIT FISH PENDANT

Bible reference: John 21

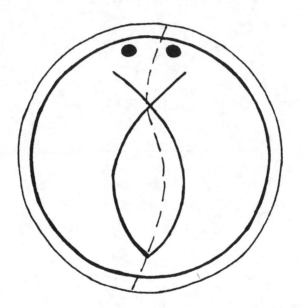

This craft will take two weeks to complete.

Each child will need
- modelling material*
- 2 cords or chains for necklaces
- cutting tool
- varnish and a brush

* There are many proprietary brands of modelling material available from craft shops or good stationers. Some dry at room temperature, others need baking in an oven. Some come in a range of colours, others need painting. For this craft you will need two colours or some paint. As an alternative to a proprietary brand you could use salt dough (see craft no. 88 for the recipe).

Follow the general instructions for the modelling material you are using. Make a disc 0.5cm thick and approximately 5cm in diameter. As you make the disc insert both chains, or make two holes for cords, 1cm apart. With a different colour (or paint these parts a different colour when appropriate) roll out a thin sausage shape. Add a border all round the rim of the disc and form a Christian fish symbol in the centre of the disc, with the head-tail line passing between the two cord holes or chains.

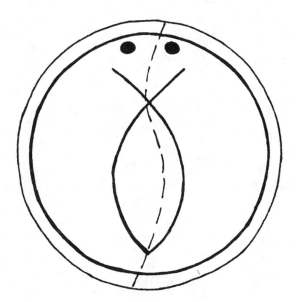

Use the cutter to divide the disc into two, cutting a zigzag line starting between the two cord holes or chains and passing through the centre of the fish. Leave to harden or bake as required and then varnish (and paint if necessary) the two necklaces the following week.

Keep one of the half necklaces and give the other to a friend, explaining how when early Christians met a stranger they would form one half of the fish symbol in the sand, identifying fellow Christians if the stranger completed the symbol.

Section Five:

SEASONAL CRAFTS

These ideas, along with those in the 'Crafts to Give' section, are more appropriate than those in the earlier sections for mid-week groups with less Bible teaching content.

If you are involved in a mid-week club for unchurched children you will almost certainly spend some time doing crafts linked to the festivals of Christmas and Easter, and special dates like Valentine's Day. Don't miss the opportunity—make sure that all of the crafts carry a Christian message home with the children.

'CHRISTMAS GIFT' FLAP-UP CARD

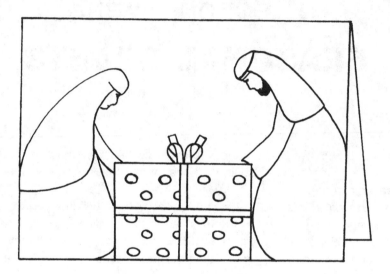

Each child will need
- an A5 sheet of thin card or thick paper*
- a piece of brightly coloured paper 7cm × 4cm
- thin paper curling ribbon
- scissors, glue, a pencil, a rubber and felt pens

* Adjust the size of the paper or card if you have envelopes that you wish the card to fit.

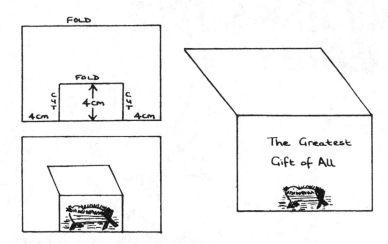

Fold the sheet of paper or card in half. Measure in 4cm from each side along the bottom of the front of the card and cut two slits 4cm long. Stick the piece of brightly coloured paper on the flap that has been formed. Cut lengths of the ribbon and stick them across the coloured paper forming a bow shape at the top, so that the flap resembles a present. Draw two simple figures of a man and a woman, kneeling either side of the present. Fold open the flap and lightly mark the edges of the flap on the inside page with the pencil. Open up the card. Draw a picture of Jesus in the manger within the area marked by the pencil. Above the marked area write 'The Greatest Gift of All' and then rub out the pencil lines.

CHRISTMAS TREE WREATHS

These tree decorations act as a reminder of the Christmas story.

Each child will need
- old Christmas cards showing nativity related scenes (if you can't collect enough appropriate old cards you may need to buy a pack of new cards)
- circles of paper approximately 10cm in diameter
- material for the borders (crêpe, tissue or shiny paper or pre-cut adhesive stars, etc.)
- cotton
- a circular frame, cut from card, with an inside diameter of 8cm
- scissors, sticky tape, glue and a pencil

Use the frame to select a picture from a card. Draw round the inside of the frame and cut out the picture circle. Mount it in the centre of a paper circle. Make a border around the picture (see suggested ideas below). Cut approximately 10cm of cotton to make a hanging loop and attach it to the back of the wreath.

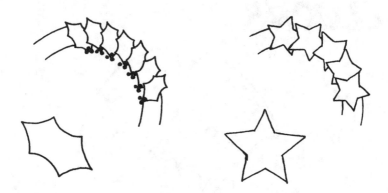

Rosette border: Cut a 2.5cm wide strip of crêpe paper. Stick it round the picture, pleating as you go.

Holly border: Cut out small holly leaves in two shades of green tissue paper. Stick them round the picture and add berries using a red felt pen.

Star border: Use gold or silver self-adhesive stars to frame the picture.

Shiny border: Cut a ring of shiny paper to frame the picture.

CHRISTMAS 'BIRTHDAY' BALLOONS

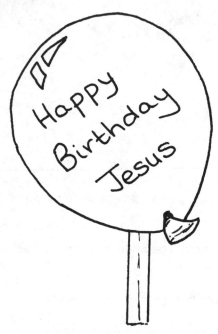

A tree decoration that acts as a reminder of why we celebrate Christmas.

Each child will need
- a piece of coloured thick paper or thin card approximately 12cm × 7cm
- a pipe-cleaner or paper-covered, metal bag-tie
- felt or metallic or glitter pens
- a balloon template cut out of card
- scissors, glue and a pencil

Draw round the template, turn it over and draw round it again. Cut out a pair of balloons. Stick the pair together, sandwiching a pipe-cleaner or bag-tie between the two halves so that 3–4cm stick out at the base of the balloon. Use the coloured, metallic or glitter pens to write 'Happy birthday Jesus' on the balloon. The balloon can now be attached to the branch of the Christmas tree, so that it stands up above the branch.

You could make a bunch of balloons using different coloured pieces of card.

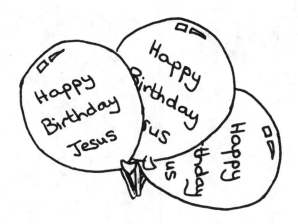

CHRISTMAS STAMP PRINT WRAPPING PAPER

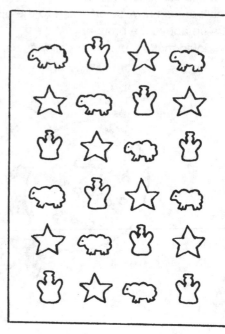

Wrapping paper that includes symbols that act as reminders of the Christmas story.

As a craft knife is used this will need close adult supervision. Younger children can be given the potato stamps already cut.

Each child will need
- an A2 sheet of paper
- 3 halves of large potatoes, cut in half lengthways
- either biscuit cutters or cardboard templates of a star, an angel and a sheep
- a craft or kitchen knife (a craft knife is preferable as the blade can be retracted when not in use)
- paint and a brush

If you have shaped biscuit cutters, push one firmly into the cut side of the potato, cutting through at least 1cm. Then, with the craft knife, slice almost 1cm off the potato in towards the cutter. When all the outside slice is removed, lift off the cutter. If you do not have an appropriate biscuit cutter, place the template on the cut side of the potato and, with the craft knife, cut straight down, at least 1cm into the potato, all round the outline. Then slice almost 1cm off the potato in to meet the downward cuts. Both methods will leave a raised pad of the shape in the centre of the potato. This can now be used as a stamp. Make the other two in the same way.

Use a brush to apply the paint to the raised shape on one stamp and print the design onto the paper. Use the different stamps and different colours to create a repeat pattern all over the sheet.

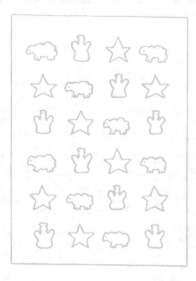

CHRISTMAS SHOE-BOX STABLE SCENE

Each child will need
- a shoe-box
- brown paper or paint
- cut-out pictures of Mary, Joseph and the baby Jesus; a donkey; an angel; shepherds and sheep*
- card (use the back of Christmas cards)
- shredded crêpe paper in brown and yellow
- scissors, glue and felt pens

* If you have a plentiful supply of old Christmas cards with nativity pictures on them let the children choose appropriate cards and cut out the pictures. Otherwise find one card for each of the required pictures and photocopy it as many times as necessary.

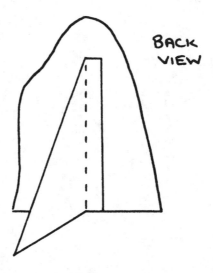

BACK VIEW

Paint the shoe-box brown, or cover it in brown paper, and stand it on its side. Either roughly cut round the pictures selected from Christmas cards or colour the photocopied pictures, stick them onto card and cut them out. Cut right-angled triangles of card just shorter than each picture. Fold a 1cm strip on the upright side of the triangle and stick that strip to the back of the picture. This will enable the picture to stand.

Place the picture of the angel on top of the box. Spread a handful of shredded paper over the floor of the box and arrange the remaining figures inside.

EPIPHANY STAR BISCUITS

These biscuits can be made before Christmas to hang on the tree or after Christmas to mark the Wise Men coming to visit Jesus.

Each child will need
- 100g plain flour
- 50g caster sugar
- 50g butter
- 1 egg yolk
- boiled sweets
- narrow ribbon
- a skewer or knitting needle
- a mixing bowl, a sieve and a fork or beater for mixing
- a baking sheet covered with greased tin foil
- access to an oven

Cream together the butter and sugar until pale. Beat in the egg yolk, sift in the flour and mix to a firm dough, adding a drop of water if necessary. If possible, wrap the dough and place it in a fridge for thirty minutes. Take pieces of dough and roll them into thin sausage shapes. Form these sausage shapes into five-pointed stars on the greased foil, so that they make a biscuit approximately 12cm across. Place a boiled sweet in the centre of each and use the skewer or knitting needle to make a hole through the biscuit at the top of one point on each star. The quantity of mixture will make about four biscuits. Cook in a preheated oven (190°C, Gas Mark 5) for about eight minutes. As soon as they come out of the oven, check that the hole still goes all the way through each biscuit and leave to cool on a rack. Thread a thin piece of ribbon through the hole.

The biscuits can either be eaten or hung on the Christmas tree as a decoration.

EPIPHANY 'THANK YOU' CARDS

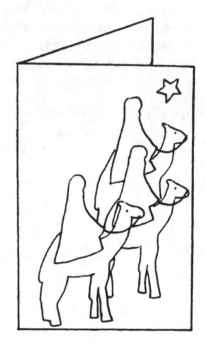

These 'thank you' cards can be made quite quickly and will act as a reminder of the gifts that the Wise Men brought Jesus.

Each child will need
- an A5 sheet of thin blue card
- a piece of light brown paper approximately 17cm × 8cm (parcel wrap would be fine)
- 3 pieces of different, brightly coloured paper approximately 5cm × 3.5cm
- a silver self-adhesive star
- camel and Wise Man templates
- scissors, glue and felt pens

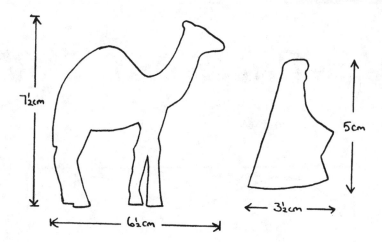

Draw round the camel template three times on brown paper and cut out. Draw round the Wise Man template on three different pieces of brightly coloured paper and cut out. Fold the card in half. Place and stick the Wise Men sitting on their camels, overlapping to fit on the card. Stick the star in the top right-hand corner. Write the Bible verse at the bottom of the left-hand page inside the card. Write 'Thank you for my gift' in the centre of the right-hand page.

Bible verse: 'They opened their treasures and presented him with gifts of gold and of incense and of myrrh' (Matthew 2:11).

VALENTINE'S DAY CARD

Bible reference: John 11:1–44

Each child will need
- an A5 sheet of thin white card
- a piece of red card approximately 15cm × 10cm
- pictures of flowers cut from a magazine or seed catalogue
- scissors, glue, a pencil and a red felt pen

Draw a heart on the red card and cut it out. Fold the white card in half and stick the heart on the front, so that the card lifts open. Cut out some small pictures of flowers and decorate the heart by sticking either a posy in the centre or flowers all round the border. Open the card and use the red pen to write, 'Jesus and I love you.'

HOLY WEEK CALENDAR

Bible reference: Mark 11–16

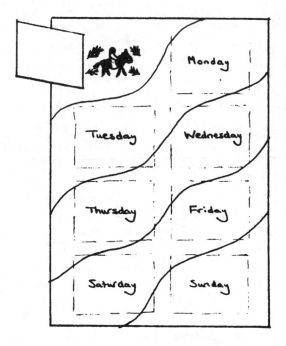

This is an advent-style calendar that the children can take home and use throughout the week leading up to Easter.

Each child will need
- an A4 sheet of white card
- an A4 sheet of paper
- scissors, a ruler, glue, a pencil, felt pens, paints and a brush

Use the pencil and ruler to mark out eight boxes, each 6cm wide × 4cm deep on the white card. The top two boxes should both start 2cm down from the top of the card and 3cm in from the sides of the card. There should be a 3cm gap between the boxes in each direction. Draw freehand wavy lines that cross the card diagonally, from lower left to upper right, separating out the boxes—the top left box, the second left and top right together, the third left and second right together, the bottom left and third right together and finally the bottom right. Paint the five areas, leaving the boxes blank. The top left stripe should be purple, the next green, the third red, the fourth black and the last yellow. Next draw pictures in the eight boxes:

- Jesus entering Jerusalem on a donkey in the top left box
- Jesus clearing the temple in the top right box
- Jesus teaching in the temple in the second left box
- Judas accepting the coins to betray Jesus
- the Lord's Supper
- the crucifixion
- the guard at the tomb
- the resurrection

From the sheet of paper cut eight rectangles 8cm × 6cm. Place them over the pictures, sticking down a 1cm strip to the left of each picture (you may need small pieces of reusable adhesive putty to keep the doors closed). Paint the paper so that it exactly matches the stripes on the card. Write in the middle of each paper door the date to be opened, starting with Palm Sunday and then one for each day of Holy Week ending with Easter Sunday. You may need to write the names on white sticky labels rather than directly on the door—especially the days where the doors are black.

EASTER FOLD-OUT CARD

Each child will need
- a sheet of thin card approximately 13cm × 30cm
- scissors, a ruler and felt pens

Measure 10cm intervals along the long side and fold the card in three so that you have two flaps that open out to the left and then to the right. Fold closed.

On the front of the card draw and colour a large black cross. On the second flap draw a stone shape that comes approximately 8cm out from the fold and approximately 10cm up from the bottom. Write on the stone 'Happy Easter' and then cut away the rest of the flap. Draw round the stone shape, so that the outline is on the back page, and then open that flap. In the stone outline write 'He is risen!' Draw colourful rays coming from the stone to the edges of the card and on the back of the stone cut-away draw flowers.

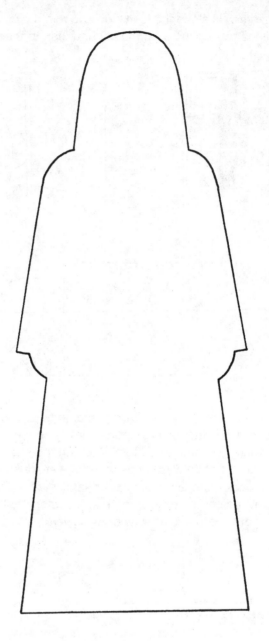

100 Simple Bible Crafts